Dialogue
WITH THE MASTER
LIFE LESSONS FOR THE GROWING CHRISTIAN

To Tanisha —
What a pleasure to meet you!
God's Best to you,
God Be Praised!
Bunnie Medley Jones

Dialogue
WITH THE MASTER
LIFE LESSONS FOR THE GROWING CHRISTIAN

BEVERLY MEDLEY JONES

© 2005 by Beverly Medley Jones. All rights reserved.

Printed in the United States of America

Packaged by Pleasant Word, a division of WinePress Publishing, PO Box 428, Enumclaw, WA 98022. The views expressed or implied in this work do not necessarily reflect those of Pleasant Word, a division of WinePress Publishing. Ultimate design, content, and editorial accuracy of this work are the responsibilities of the author.

No part of this publication may be reproduced, stored in a retrieval system, or transmitted in any way by any means—electronic, mechanical, photocopy, recording, or otherwise—without the prior permission of the copyright holder, except as provided by USA copyright law.

Unless otherwise noted, all Scriptures are taken from the Holy Bible, New International Version, Copyright © 1973, 1978, 1984 by the International Bible Society. Used by permission of Zondervan Publishing House. The "NIV" and "New International Version" trademarks are registered in the United States Patent and Trademark Office by International Bible Society.

Scripture references marked KJV are taken from the King James Version of the Bible.

Verses marked NKJV are taken from the New King James Version, © 1979, 1980, 1982 by Thomas Nelson, Inc., Publishers. Used by permission.

Verses marked AMP are taken from The Amplified Bible, Old Testament, © 1965 and 1987 by The Zondervan Corporation, and from The Amplified New Testament, © 1954, 1958, 1987 by The Lockman Foundation. Used by permission.

ISBN 1-4141-0367-0
Library of Congress Catalog Card Number: 2004195522

To Roger, my best friend and my strongest supporter.

To Brandon and Bryan, always the apples of my eye.

To Diamond and Seannita, you will forever be in my heart.

Table of Contents

Preface 9

Part I: How to Be Sure

Chapter 1: Come to the Table, It's Dinnertime! 13
Chapter 2: Who's Your Daddy? 17
Chapter 3: Making the Connection 21
Chapter 4: Savor the Flavor of Christ 25
Chapter 5: Open Your Gifts 29

Inspiration: My New Life Commitments 34

Part II: Growing Up in Christ

Chapter 6: Cover Up 37
Chapter 7: Who Lights Your Fire? 41
Chapter 8: A Bird Feeder, Lord? 45
Chapter 9: Take Out the Garbage 49
Chapter 10: "Don't Be No Punk" 53

Inspiration: Like A Child 58

Part III: Surrender in Worship

Chapter 11: Good Is Not Good Enough 63
Chapter 12: Downtime 65
Chapter 13: Talk To the Hand! 67
Chapter 14: Assume a Position 71
Chapter 15: God's Presents or God's Presence? 75

Inspiration: If God Would Answer "Why" 79

Part IV: Living the Good Life

Chapter 16: Remote Control God 83
Chapter 17: Bear, Just Bear 87
Chapter 18: Wood, Hay, and Stubble 91
Chapter 19: Grease the Wheels 95

Inspiration: For You Who Helped Me Grow 98

Part V: We Win!

Chapter 20: It's Not What You Know,
   It's Who You Know 101
Chapter 21: Going All the Way 107
Chapter 22: Survive or Live? 111
Chapter 23: We're On a Roll! 115
Chapter 24: Live in the Light 119

Inspiration: Woman of Destiny 123

Preface

I drive on a scenic parkway every day on my way to work. On one particularly gorgeous autumn morning I was so enthralled by the breath-taking view that I promised myself that immediately after my last student left, I would leave school and go directly to the park. I couldn't wait to experience up close the beauty I had seen from the road.

I parked the car with anticipation of enjoying the afternoon. I walked directly toward the area that had so captured my attention from afar. As I walked, I began to see what was really in the park—dead leaves, dried-up sticks, horse manure, sharp rocks, decaying tree trunks, and stagnant water. The scene up close was the antithesis of the majestic beauty I had beheld from far away.

Life, up close, can often show the ugliness of our flaws, failures, disappointments, and the many battles that come our way. We can become discouraged looking only at our immediate part of the picture. Our difficulties may be repulsive while we're in the midst of them, but God sees the finished product, and He knows how to make our lives a beautiful sight. He sees the entire scene—the panoramic view of our lives. Like my scenic view from the road, God sees how all the parts combine to form a beautiful picture of His children.

Part I

How to Be Sure

CHAPTER 1

Come to the Table, It's Dinnertime!

When I was a little girl, I could be found most days playing somewhere around my neighborhood. It was much safer for children to play away from home when I was growing up in the 60s than it is now. I could be on the next corner or at a friend's house two streets over, and my parents knew I'd be all right. A neighborhood ritual was for the moms to go out on the back steps and call their children home at dinnertime. When I heard that distinctive voice yelling, "Be———-ver————lyyyy!" I knew what I had to do, and I came a-running. It was dinnertime!

Each child in my neighborhood recognized his or her own mother's voice as she called her children home. No matter how many children there were with the same name, never an error was made when they responded to their own mother's call to dinner.

Thinking back, I remember not hesitating to answer Mom's call. For one thing, I knew I'd be in trouble if she had to call me again. But more importantly, I knew that what she was calling me in for was going to be good. She had taken time to prepare a delicious meal for her family, and I was truly going to enjoy it.

God has prepared some special meals for His children, and He's calling us to come in—it's dinnertime! In Mark 2:17, Jesus tells us that He has not called the righteous, but sinners to repentance. Every time a sinner hears about Jesus, that's the Father calling him or her to the table. Just as the calls of the moms told us neighborhood kids to come in, the call of Jesus to the world is "Come." In John 6:37, Jesus lets us know that we can come to Him and be welcome, and He will "in no wise cast out" those who respond to His call.

As I recall coming in the house for dinner, I was greeted with the command from my mother, "Wash your hands." Our Father has a plan to wash us, as He has told us in Revelation 1:5: "Unto Him that loved us, and washed us from our sins in his own blood." The washing God wants to do is the removal of the stain of sin, which can only be done through the perfect sacrifice, the shedding of Jesus' blood at Calvary. Once we receive Jesus as our Savior and believe on His death and resurrection, we are cleansed from our sin and received by Him.

Like most children, I wet my hands and ran to the table, ready to begin. But my mother, knowing that in my haste I hadn't done a sufficient cleansing job, would ultimately send me back to wash again, "And use soap!" Titus 3:5 describes the "soap" God uses daily with His children.

"Not by works of righteousness which we have done, but according to His mercy He saved us, by the washing of regeneration, and renewing of the Holy Ghost." God is telling us that we can't wash ourselves, but He makes us clean, makes us new, and has sent the Holy Ghost to "scrub" out the old man and reveal the new creation in Christ.

Once I finally got to the table, what's the first thing I did? Like most children, I got up on my knees so I could see my plate, my family, and the meal that was set before me. On our knees is where the Father wants us to be so that we can receive the feast He has for us. "Thou preparest a table before me in the presence of mine enemies, thou anointest my head with oil, my cup runneth over" (Psalm 23:5). It is from our knees in prayer and earnest listening that God can reveal the spread of promise and blessing He has for us. Jeremiah 29:12–13 says, "Then shall ye call upon me, and ye shall go and pray unto me, and I will hearken unto you. And ye shall seek me, and find me, when ye shall search for me with all your heart." Through prayer and meditation in His Word, God will show us His plan for our victory as He orders our steps.

So, what's for dinner? Jesus has stirred up all our favorites, too numerous to count. I'll name just a few:

1. Bread: "And Jesus said unto them, I am the bread of life: he that cometh to me shall never hunger: and he that believeth in me shall never thirst" (John 6:35).

2. Water: "But whosoever drinketh of the water that I shall give him shall never thirst again; but the water that I shall give him shall be in him a well of water springing up into everlasting life" (John 4:14).

3. Fruit: "But the fruit of the Spirit is love, joy, peace, longsuffering, gentleness, goodness, faith, meekness, temperance, against such there is no law" (Galatians 5:22–23).

4. Milk: "As newborn babes, desire the sincere milk of the Word, that ye may grow thereby" (1 Peter 2:2).

Life is at the table. John 10:10 tells us that Jesus has come to give us life, and life more abundantly. This includes every promise God has made to His children—salvation, health, prosperity, wisdom, favor, and that He hears and answers every prayer we pray. "He that hath the Son hath life; and he that hath not the Son of God hath not life" (1 John 5:12). For the child of God, the table is set with all the blessings that come with fellowship with the Father. Not that we won't ever have problems, but just as God prepared a table for David in the presence of his enemies in Psalm 23, He will nourish and fill us even when the hard times come. He will walk us through the dangers, and we can come out healthy and strong in Him.

It's dinnertime! Come to the table God has prepared for you. God is calling us to come in and receive the feast of His presence, His goodness, and His blessing. "Faithful is He that calleth you, who also will do it" (1 Thessalonians 5:24).

CHAPTER 2

Who's Your Daddy?

Remember when kids used to pretend to wrestle and the winner made the loser, who was usually pinned or in a headlock, say *uncle*? I was often involved in those mini-conflicts as a child as a spectator or a participant, and I fully understood the message of concession expressed by the word *uncle*.

Recently, I watched two neighbor boys wrestling in the backyard. Just as the victor pinned his victim, and I waited to hear him cry *uncle*, the winner grunted, "Who's your daddy?" The loser issued a muffled, "You are," past the forearm that was wrapped around his neck. I gather that "Who's your daddy" is some kind of victory chant kids use today. Though stunned at the crudeness, I thought about the practicality of finding the real answer to this question.

When we are in trouble, being strangled by the enemy who has our arms twisted behind our backs—that's the time we should ask ourselves, "Who's your daddy?" We do indeed have a daddy—a heavenly Father who wants to show himself strong on our behalf.

Daddy, from the eyes of his child, is a hero. He is *strong*—he can pick up anything, he can loosen lids, unstick doors, and carry boxes. He is the *protector*—he can beat up everybody and he is not afraid of anything or anybody. He is *smart*—he knows how to do everything. He can teach his children to ride a bike, build a birdhouse, fish, and play any sport. He is *loving*, and even if he is not one to show affection physically, he still communicates his love in subtle messages. A good dad will kill for his child; a good dad will die for his child.

The pattern for fatherhood is confirmed in the example from our heavenly Father. Isaiah 41:10 tells us how God's *strong* arm will uphold us. Our Lord, the Shepherd, is our *protector*, "Yea, though I walk through the valley of the shadow of death, I will fear no evil for Thou art with me" (Psalm 23:4). And when it comes to being *smart*, 1 Corinthians 1:25 shows us, "Because the foolishness of God is wiser than men; and the weakness of God is stronger than men." God is so wise that He uses preaching, considered foolishness to the world, to express a mystery so astounding that it confounds the worldly wise. He knows our hearts, minds, motives, thoughts, and intentions. David reminds us that Father God knew us before we were born. "For You formed my inward parts; You covered me in my mother's womb" (Psalm 139:13, NKJV).

God showed His profound *love* for us when He came to earth as Jesus, the Son who gave His life, not for His own crimes—because He is perfect—but to pay for our sins. "Greater love has no one than this, that one lay down his life for his friends" (John 15:13, NIV). In 1 John 4:7–10 we find that love is the very essence of God. "God is love."

The most rewarding feeling a daddy has is when his child wants to be just like him. God's proudest moment, too, is when His children desire to be like Him. **The Father came to earth in the form of Jesus the Son to be an example of who He is. His death and resurrection made it possible** for us to enter into His family as His children, and His Holy Spirit enables us to live obediently, as Christ did. That's the gospel in a nutshell. God's will for us is that we first believe His gospel message, repent of our sins, and accept Jesus as Savior and Lord. Then, through the Holy Spirit, He begins the process of conforming us into the image of His Son (Romans 8:29).

Contrary to the espousal of many religions, not everyone is God's child! As touching and tolerant as the phrase, "We're all God's children" sounds, nothing could be further from the truth. We are indeed all creations of God, but Jesus made the truth clear in John 8:42 and 44. Jesus rebuked the Pharisees, the religious leaders of His day, by telling these hypocrites that their father was the devil. Only those who love Jesus and have surrendered their lives to Him can have God as Father.

We know what God is like. We have examples through His Word, Jesus, and our earthly fathers. Now, it's time to see who belongs to the Heavenly Father. Take this paternity test:

1. Do I look like Him? Do I walk in the sinful works of the flesh (Galatians 5:19–21) or in the fruit of the Spirit of God (Galatians 5:22–24)?

2. Do I belong to His family? Do I believe, and have I received Jesus as my Savior (John 1:12)? Does God recognize me as His child (Romans 8:15–16)?

3. Do I talk like Him? Are my words uplifting (Ephesians 4:29)? Do I express holy thoughts (Philippians 4:8)?

4. Do I walk like Him? Do I forgive (Matthew 6:14)? Am I a doer of His Word (James 1:22)?

5. Do I brag about Him through my testimony and in witnessing to others? Do I trust Him to provide for and protect me?

Whoever answers yes to these questions can say, "My Daddy is the Lord!"

> *"Can a woman forget her sucking child that she should not have compassion on the son of her womb? Yea, she may forget, yet will I not forget thee. Behold, I have graven thee upon the palms of my hands, thy walls are continually before me."*
> (Isaiah 49:15–16)

Love,
Your Father.

CHAPTER 3

Making the Connection

My husband Roger and I dabble in the real estate market. We buy and rehab houses and either resell them or rent them. One evening, as our family was working on a house, our son Bryan picked up the receiver of the wall phone and began dialing. "Hello, hello, hello." Nothing. To his chagrin, he received no response to his greetings. The phone line had not yet been activated, and no signals were getting through. This was news to Bryan, but we know that we can dial all we want and talk all we want, but we won't get through unless we're *connected*. This concept is no different in our spiritual lives. We must be connected in order to hear from God or to be heard by Him.

How do we connect with God? Is there a connector, a link? Yes, there is. He is called the Mediator in 1 Timothy 2:5. He is called the Way in John 14:6. His name is Jesus, and He tells us, "No one comes to the Father except through me" (NKJV).

There are many who believe that God hears the prayers of sinners. I can recall times before I was saved that I "prayed" that God would get me out of the messes I had gotten myself into. When He brought me through those times, I mistakenly thought that He had answered my prayers. In reality, I had received *mercy* from God, the show of His goodness that eventually drew me toward repentance (Romans 2:4). Scripture clearly teaches that God does not hear the prayers of sinners. "For the eyes of the Lord are on the righteous and His ears are attentive to their prayer, but the face of the Lord is against those who do evil" (1 Peter 3:12). Furthermore, John 9:31 restates what had already been taught in the Old Testament, "God heareth not sinners."

Since God does not hear the prayers of sinners, what is the first prayer He *will* hear? Think about when Jesus walked this earth. John the Baptist had come before Him preaching repentance (Mark 1:4). Jesus' first recorded messages as He began His ministry were, "Repent: for the kingdom of heaven is at hand" (Matthew 4:17), and "Repent, and believe in the gospel" (Mark 1:15, NKJV). The first prayer God heard from me was my prayer of repentance—when I admitted to being a sinner in need of a Savior, asked for forgiveness, and turned from my sin. *If you haven't prayed a prayer of repentance, God hasn't heard you yet.*

As we repent, believe on Jesus as the perfect sacrifice for our sins, and ask Him to come into our hearts, the connection is made. We are connected to God. Paul, in Romans 11, terms it "grafted in" by believing on Jesus. We are now children of God who can communicate with Him as our Father. As Hebrews 4:16 invites us, "Let us therefore come boldly unto the throne of grace, that we may obtain mercy, and find grace to help in time of need."

When I pray, I use this pattern:

P—Praise. Acknowledge Who God is. (Hebrews 11:6)

C—Confession. Admit the sin that comes between God and me. (1 John 1:9)
I—Intercession. Pray for others. (James 5:16)
S—Supplication. Pray for my needs. (Matthew 6:8)
T—Thanksgiving. Thank God for what He has done and will do. (1 Chronicles 16:8)

My P-CIST method reminds me to *persist* in prayer, to ask and keep on asking, to seek and keep on seeking, to knock and keep on knocking; or as Jesus commanded, to pray without ceasing.

Making the connection means getting and keeping open communication with God. Jeremiah 33:3 is often referred to as God's telephone number, "Call unto Me and I will answer thee and show thee great and mighty things which thou knowest not."

CHAPTER 4

Savor the Flavor of Christ

Food is good isn't it? Have you ever noticed that every culture on earth involves food in their celebrations, holidays, feasts, and ceremonies? Food is essential for our nourishment, growth, and health. It also helps us relax and enjoy pleasant conversations, and often mealtime gives us the opportunity to quiet ourselves after the activity of the day.

God's Word speaks often about food. In the Garden of Eden, God put all the trees for food except that one, the forbidden tree of the knowledge of good and evil (Genesis 2:16–17). During the Exodus from Egypt, Israel was fed manna by God himself (Exodus 16:14–15, 35). Jesus responded to our need for food when He fed the five thousand (Matthew 14:19–21) and again the four thousand (Matthew 15:34–38). So there is no doubt that we do experience the need for food and we do enjoy consuming it.

God also refers to the food for the spirit. Jesus, in the wilderness (Matthew 4:4), countered Satan's temptation by proclaiming that ". . . Man shall not live by bread alone, but by every word that proceedeth out from the mouth of God (KJV)." Jesus calls himself the Bread of Life (John 6:48–51). But how are we to eat this Bread?

In John 6:53–66, Jesus wanted His disciples to eat His body and drink His blood. Many of them left Him because this requirement was too difficult for them to perform. Only twelve men stayed with Him. Those who left Jesus understood what He meant by eating His body and drinking His blood. These were Jewish people who understood that Jesus wanted to make a blood covenant with them. They knew the history of the covenant God had made with Abraham—how Abraham had been put to sleep and an animal was cut up and God walked between the pieces. In American culture, children may become "blood brothers" by mingling their blood as a sign of best friendship. But in the Jewish tradition, the blood covenant was a commitment for life. The pieces of the animal represented, essentially, the covenant partners, saying, "If I break this promise, may the same thing happen to me that has happened to this animal." Not everybody who heard Jesus make the request to partake in covenant with Him wanted to make such a serious commitment.

Think about this—Jesus was cut up and bleeding when He gave His life for us. This is the covenant promise from God. If we don't hold up our end of the covenant by believing that Jesus died for our sins and rose again and by receiving Him as our Savior, a far worse fate awaits us. John 3:18 tells us that whoever does not believe in Him is condemned already.

We take our first bite of the Bread of Life when we accept His sacrifice for our sins. At that point, we are ready to receive the nourishment we need to grow spiritually. We find this nourishment in the Word of God. Jesus is the Word, as explained in John 1:14, "And the Word was made flesh and dwelt among us . . . ." Just as with physical food, there are different kinds of spiritual foods. In 1 Peter 2:2–3, we are told:

"As newborn babes, desire the sincere milk of the word, that ye may grow thereby: If so be ye have tasted that the Lord is gracious." As we grow in wisdom and understanding, we can begin to dive into the deeper truths of God's Word, referred to as "meat" (1 Corinthians 3:2). Just as certain physical foods are known to be especially good for us—such as fruits and vegetables—so the Word is essential to build us up and develop us into the image of Christ. Colossians 3:16 tells us, to "let the Word of Christ dwell richly in you," which will benefit every part of our being.

The major difference between physical and spiritual food is its effect on us. The more physical food we eat, the less hungry we get. But the more spiritual food we eat from God's Word, the hungrier we get for more!

Feed yourself. "O taste and see that the Lord is good . . ." (Psalm 34:8).

As you grow, you will certainly savor the flavor of Christ.

CHAPTER 5

Open Your Gifts

Once I heard a story about a man who died and went to heaven. In heaven, he was shown a room full of beautifully wrapped gifts of all shapes and sizes. Mesmerized, he asked the angel what fortunate person was to receive all those fabulous gifts. The angel responded, "These were all supposed to be yours while you were on earth, but you never asked for them."

We, indeed, have gifts we are to receive from God the Father. These gifts are intended to help us live a joyful, victorious, fulfilling life. Wouldn't it be a shame to find out after it's too late that we could have avoided lots of pitfalls and lived a more successful life if only we had used every gift God has made available for our benefit? This year, make it your purpose to open your gifts!

I recall one Christmas my twin sons wanted a particular video game system. In shopping for this, I noticed that the main component, which was quite pricey, also required an assortment of accessories (which, of course, cost extra) in order work properly. The cords, controllers, and games began to out-price the system itself, and then, of course, I had to buy a television to play it all on!

I began to think of the joy I would experience as I watched my boys unwrap this set of gifts. Our Father must feel that kind of joy as He sees His children receive the precious gifts He has for us.

Like that game system, God offers all people His "main component." Romans 6:23 says, "the gift of God is eternal life through Jesus Christ our Lord." As we accept Jesus as Savior and Lord of our lives, we are assured of forgiveness of our sins and the promise to live forever in heaven with God. Unless we receive the gift of Jesus and His sacrifice for our sins, we are not eligible to receive the other promises (or accessories) that come only to members of the family of Christ.

Once we become children of God, Jesus has more "under the tree" for us besides eternity in heaven. In John 10:10, Jesus tells us that He has come to give us life, and life more abundantly. This means that life on this earth will be more abundant, rich, blessed.

What is a gift? In the Greek language, the word for gift, *charisma*, means gratuity, deliverance, endowment, or qualification. These are what I call the accessories—the extras—that come with walking with Jesus and having a relationship with Him. These are the gifts for living, those that help us in this life on earth.

Gratuity: This is the tip we give to a waiter at a restaurant who stands in our presence and waits until we tell him what to do. The waiter who deserves a tip is very patient, does not tell us what he wants us to order, but graciously accepts whatever we request and puts forth his best efforts to serve us. In Isaiah 40:31, God tips His waiters. "But they that wait upon the Lord shall renew their strength; they shall mount up with wings as eagles; they shall run, and not be weary; and they shall walk, and not faint." This verse is often used to encourage us to be patient. The word "wait" here does not refer to the passage of time but rather staying in the presence of God awaiting instructions, much like the waiter does at a restaurant. Through prayer, meditation in the Word, and quiet listening, we wait to hear from God. The tip we receive here is renewed *strength*. God promises that as we spend time in His presence, we shall be as eagles. Just as the eagle can fly hundreds of miles from its home and always finds its way back, so God will give us *direction*, always leading us in the right path.

God also promises *endurance*, the ability to hold on, not give up. Just as a runner who has trained properly can finish the race, we who receive training from the Lord will receive divine perseverance to complete each task He gives us, being confident that He who hath begun a good work in us "will perform it until the day of Jesus Christ" (Philippians 1:6,).

Note that in Isaiah 40:31, God proclaims that we shall walk and not faint. This refers to His ability to help us remain faithful. Through all the temptations and disappointments this life's walk presents, our Father is faithful to see that we do not suffer beyond what we can stand and to provide a way of escape so that we are able to bear it (1 Corinthians 10:13). *Faithfulness*, the ability to go through life at a steady pace while remaining committed and obedient to God, is a promise He gives to those who wait on Him. Open your gift of strength and receive direction, endurance, and faithfulness.

Deliverance: I compare this to the job of a letter carrier who delivers packages from one place to another. God desires to bring us from our present place in life and place us at a higher level. As we are reminded in 2 Corinthians 3:18, "But we all, with open face beholding as in a glass the glory of the Lord, are changed into the same image from glory to glory, even as by the Spirit of the Lord." In Psalm 91:1, God tells us where He wants to bring us. "He that dwelleth in the secret place of the most High shall abide under the shadow of the Almighty." The Father's desire is for His children to have a closer, deeper, more intimate relationship with Him.

Psalm 91:3 speaks of deliverance in a slightly different vein. "Surely he shall deliver thee from the snare of the fowler and from the noisome pestilence." This refers to protection from the dangers that await us in this life. As I researched this verse, I found that a snare, as referred to here, was a trap set on the ground by fowlers, or bird-hunters. As birds wandered around looking for food, they were netted or caged by these snares. The enemy, Satan, seeks to trap God's people in like fashion. If we find ourselves looking in the wrong direction—down at ground level—for our food (that which satisfies our needs or desires), we can also be snared. The enemy will present an easy out, a quick fix, fast cash, or some other scheme we think will supply our needs, which we later discover was meant to destroy us. We should look to God for our needs, as Psalm 121:2 says, because all our help comes from the Lord. Open your gift of deliverance!

Endowment: To endow means to provide. We know from Philippians 4:19 that God will supply all our needs according to His riches in glory by Christ Jesus. Abraham found when he was told to sacrifice his son, Isaac, on the altar in obedience to God, that God is Jehovah Jireh, the Lord our Provider. A ram caught in the bushes was God's *provision* for the sacrifice so that Isaac could be spared.

Many depend on the lottery, the government, popularity, talent, or appearance, a job, or various systems in society to provide their needs. I personally discovered God's provision when I was told that my teaching position would be eliminated. I found myself out of the profession within two years. The words of Jesus in Matthew 6:33 began to ring in my mind. "But seek ye first the kingdom of God, and his righteousness; and all these things shall be added unto you." I began to realize that my Provider does not want me to worry about food, clothing, shelter, or any other need. Then one day while in prayer, in my heart I heard God whisper these words, "Just as you must be willing to lose your life for my sake to gain it, you must also be willing to lose your livelihood to gain your Source." That revelation made clear to me that God wants to show himself strong on my behalf by being my provider. Open your gift of provision!

Qualification: When one has qualifications, he or she is eligible for some position or recognition. To have *eligibility* one must pass certain requirements. God's Word tells us that every child of God is eligible to receive the promises He has made. The eligibility requirements are outlined in John 1:12, "But as many as received him, to them gave he power to become the sons of God, even to them that believe on his name." Two requirements appear here: *receive* and *believe*. Receive Jesus as Lord of your life, the one whose blood atoned for your sins as He died on the cross. Believe that He rose from the dead and is alive, and then trust Him to be with you daily. For those eligible, Jesus gives the power (the right) to become a member of God's family.

In Romans 8:15–17, the apostle Paul explains that we are heirs of God and joint heirs with Christ. When I think of being an heir, I think of wanting to get my share of the riches. Don't you think it's time we take hold of the family fortune? Open your gift of eligibility.

This year, make it your goal to receive *all* the gifts God has for you. Walk as His child, His heir. Get your strength in Him. Get your deliverance in Him. Get all your needs provided by Him. Recognize that all your ability comes from the Father God. Remember James 1:17, "Every good gift and every perfect gift is from above, and cometh down from the Father of Lights, with whom is no variableness, neither shadow of turning."

My New Life Commitments

IN THE BEGINNING OF MY NEW LIFE:
I will commit myself to the Lord. *Psalm 37: 5*

IN THE BEGINNING OF MY NEW LIFE:
I will trust in the Lord. *Proverbs 3: 5–6*

IN THE BEGINNING OF MY NEW LIFE:
I will study God's Word. *John 15:7*

IN THE BEGINNING OF MY NEW LIFE:
I will pray, and pray, and pray. *Mark 11:24*

IN THE BEGINNING OF MY NEW LIFE:
I will choose to do right. *Colossians 3:17*

> Colossians 3:10:
>
> And have put on the new man, which is renewed in knowledge after the image of him that created him.

PART II

Growing Up in Christ

CHAPTER 6

Cover Up

In the area of the Midwest where I live, fall often introduces itself severely. I notice around late September that it begins to get very cold very quickly. I watch the last of my tomato crop and check it against the weather reports. When I hear there is a chance of frost, I race outside to cover my harvest because I have learned from former losses that the plants I cover survive, and the ones I don't, don't. Reflection on this seasonal ritual leads me to ask this question: Why do we cover things?

> **Protection.** We want to keep our property and ourselves from being destroyed by damaging elements. We use an umbrella to protect us from the rain, a coat to protect us from the cold; our roof protects us from the turbulent weather. Even our furniture might be covered as a barrier against the damage that accompanies our kids, pets, and guests.

Comfort. My children often come to me to receive the comforter of all hurt children, the Band-aid. Even for microscopic injuries, the plastic strip is a silent voice that proclaims that healing is on the way. And who hasn't lifted a hand to shade eyes from the brightness of the sun? We use a blanket, even when it's not cold, as a covering to comfort us as we rest.

Security. What would life be like if we didn't have windows or doors? Thieves could ransack our homes at will. Wild creatures could set up residency, leaving in their wake injury and disease. Every storm raging outside would have full occupancy inside our dwellings. We do not hesitate to cover our doorways and window openings so that we can rest inside knowing we have security from potential dangers that lurk outside our homes.

God wants us to cover up for these same reasons. He wants to cover us and *be* our covering.

The first covering is demonstrated at creation. Genesis 2 tells us that God did not cause it to rain at first, "but a mist went up from the earth and watered the whole face of the ground" (Genesis 2:6). Then, in Noah's time, as mankind became increasingly wicked, God removed His covering and allowed the rains and the fountains to destroy life on earth. In Genesis 7:11-12 (NKJV), we see ". . . on that day all the fountains of the great deep were broken up, and the windows of heaven were opened. And the rain was on the earth forty days and forty nights." The mist, which had been supplied by God as a covering for nourishment, protection, comfort, and security was removed with the result of total destruction upon the earth.

Cover Up

David, the Psalmist, often referred to the covering God provides for His children. "O God the Lord, the strength of my salvation, You have covered my head [my mind, my thoughts] in the day of battle" (Psalm 140:7, NKJV).

Another name used for covering is "refuge," as in refugees who come into a country to receive protection and security, to be "covered" by that country. Psalm 46 shows us many ways to benefit from the covering God provides. "God is our refuge and strength, a very present help in trouble. Therefore we will not fear, even though the earth be removed, and though the mountains be carried into the midst of the sea" (Psalm 46:1–2, NKJV). Have we seen destruction? As the world recalls 9/11, our country saw mountains fall, and experienced economic and emotional earthquakes on a national scale. "Though its waters roar and be troubled, though the mountains shake with its swelling" (verse 3). Has anything in your world been shaken lately? Cover up.

God's covering gives us comfort. "Be still, and know that I am God; I will be exalted among the nations, I will be exalted in the earth! The Lord of hosts is with us; The God of Jacob is our refuge" (Psalm 46:10–11, NKJV).

How do we receive this protection, comfort, and security which is the divine refuge, God's covering? Remember Noah? After the removal of the covering of mist came the destruction, but after the destruction came a promise. In Genesis 9, God made a promise, a covenant with mankind, that He would never again destroy the earth by flood (Genesis 9:11–12). In verse 13, God set the rainbow in the sky as a sign of His promise. So for us, instead of the original mist that had once been a covering for the earth, we now have a covenant, a promise of protection, security, and comfort.

In the Old Testament, God gave the Ten Commandments and the Law through Moses as His covenant to the people. But we couldn't keep our end of the covenant, so God came to earth in the form of a man, our Lord Jesus, to establish a new covenant with us. Through His sacrifice on the cross, Jesus sealed in His blood God's eternal promise to cover us who believe on Him as our Savior. Through relationship with Jesus, we receive the covering—the protection, comfort, and security—and every promise in God's Word!

So, cover up. Receive protection in storms, from the thief (the devil) who wishes to steal from you, kill, and destroy you (John 10:10), comfort in dark times, and the security in knowing that joy comes in the morning. As Psalm 91 encourages us, "abide under the shadow of the Almighty." Draw close to God and allow Him to cover you with his covenant blessings of protection, comfort, and security.

CHAPTER 7

Who Lights Your Fire?

During one of our many Lake Erie spring thunderstorms, our family found ourselves sitting in complete darkness. The electricity had gone out, and I was charged with the task of finding another source of light for our household. With the predictable absence of usable batteries, the flashlights were worthless. Then it came to me—candles! They always work. I rummaged through the "everything" drawer in the kitchen and found the candles. Some were cracked, some were warped, some were still wrapped in their plastic sleeves. All were welcomed.

As I think of the heroic function the candles performed in our home that night, I am reminded of the similar roles people play on this planet. The candle is made up of the wax, the wick, and the flame. The person consists of the body, the soul, and the spirit. Let's look for a moment at the spiritual implications of such an unlikely comparison.

> 1a. The Wax—the holder for the wick. The wax is consumed as the candle continues in its service.

1b. The Body—the earthly container for the soul and spirit. The body, too, is consumed in time. "For we know that if our earthly house of this tabernacle were dissolved, we have a building of God, an house not made with hands, eternal in the heavens" (II Corinthians 5:1).

2a. The Wick—makes a candle a candle rather than a useless piece of wax. The wick makes a connection between the wax and the flame possible.

2b. The Soul—makes us human, different from the animals. "And the Lord God formed man of the dust of the ground and breathed into his nostrils the breath of life; and man became a living soul" (Genesis 2:7). We use the soul—the mind, the will, and the emotions—to express ourselves to each other and to God. This is also the part of us that can choose to do right or wrong. That's why we are admonished in Romans 12:2, "And be not conformed unto this world: but be ye transformed by the renewing of your mind, that ye may prove what is that good, and acceptable, and perfect, will of God."

3a. The Flame—makes the candle *useful*. As long as the candle sits in a drawer, it does no one any service. Only when fire is applied can the candle be ready for use.

3b. The Spirit—makes us eternal beings, useful for God's purpose. The spirit is the "real me" part of us that will live forever. My pastor, the Rev. Dr. Roland H. Crowder, used to say, "We'll all live forever, but the quality of life will be determined by what we do with

Jesus." The Bible puts it this way in John 3:18, "He that believeth on Him is not condemned: but he that believeth not is condemned already, because he hath not believed in the name of the only begotten Son of God."

A candle can be used in a variety of ways. It can give needed light, keep us from stumbling, or help us do work. It can also cause great destruction to lives and property. The difference in whether a candle (or a life) is useful or destructive is often dependent upon *who lights the flame*. Our spirit must be ignited by God through our relationship with Jesus. According to Romans 8:15–16, the Spirit of God proves to our spirit (inner, eternal self) that we are children of God. But our flesh (sinful nature) fights against the Spirit of God. Our *will* determines whether the flesh or the Spirit wins. The apostle Paul demonstrated this dilemma in Romans 7:14–25, as his sinful nature, with its desires for evil, warred against his renewed spirit, which saw its delight in the law of the Lord. But he proclaims victory in Romans 8:1, "There is therefore now no condemnation to them which are in Christ Jesus, who walk not after the flesh, but after the Spirit."

I once saw on my television listings a show called "Will and Grace." I don't know if the characters on that show are at all alike, but in the spiritual realm, will and grace are direct opposites. My will is to want what I want, to assert my rights, to do whatever moves me because I deserve to have what I want. Grace comes from God. His grace is to give me what He wants for me. Grace is God recognizing that we *don't* deserve His goodness, but because of His love for us, we receive it anyway. "For by grace are ye saved through faith; and that not of yourselves: it is the gift of God: Not of works, lest any man should boast" (Ephesians 2:8–9).

The human will leads to downfall and destruction. "There is a way which seemeth right unto a man, but the end thereof are the ways of death" (Proverbs 14:12). God's grace leads to life and peace. Jesus, in the Garden of Gethsemane, prayed, ". . . not my will, but thine be done" (Luke 22:42). At that moment, after admitting that He would rather not "drink this cup" of the agony of crucifixion, Jesus nevertheless submitted to His Father's sovereign plan. Jesus chose to continue in God's will and be the sacrifice for our sins. As His cross was lifted up at Calvary, Jesus was fulfilling His destiny as the light of the world, the flame that had been ignited by the Holy Spirit to give light to the whole world.

Let us be like the candle, allowing God to set us on fire by His Holy Spirit. Let us submit to His will and walk in His grace. As God lights the flame, the light goes up and illuminates even the darkest corners of our world. If the enemy lights the flame with sin and fleshly desires, the fire damages, destroys, and injures us as well as those around us. As we yield to God, His Spirit can burn through us and cause others to be drawn to His light. "Let your light so shine before men, that they may see your good works, and glorify your Father which is in heaven" (Matthew 5:16).

CHAPTER 8

A Bird Feeder, Lord?

My son, Brandon, came home from second grade one day with the idea that he wanted to make a bird feeder. You know the kind—a plastic, one-gallon milk jug with a big square cut out of the front. Well, he decorated it with colored markers and various household materials and tied twine around the top. Then he ushered me out to the pear tree in the back yard and pointed to his chosen branch. As I tied the final knot, Brandon yelled, "Wait, Mommy, we forgot to fill it!' Oh yeah, without the birdseed, the bird feeder is useless. It's just a pretty, but worthless, decoration, obstructing the birds' view of the real food in the pear tree.

As I recently thought about our project, I heard the Lord whisper to my mind, *Beverly, you're a bird feeder.* A what? *Lord, where is this going?* I wondered. God, in His wisdom, would show me through His Word what He meant.

Before it became a bird feeder, our jug was used for something else. It had to be emptied out and cleaned before beginning the process of becoming what we wanted it to be.

Likewise, as we repent of our sins and allow Jesus to wash them away with His cleansing blood, we start on our way to becoming the instrument God wants us to be. Just as the jug could not clean itself, neither can we. "Not by works of righteousness which we have done, but according to his mercy he saved us, by the washing of regeneration, and renewing of the Holy Ghost" (Titus 3:5).

Now the cutting begins. The process of cutting the jug is a tedious one because sometimes the jug moves and extraneous cuts can occur. As God "cuts" us, He is pruning and molding us. It is crucial that we stand still during the cutting phase. God cuts out the sins that keep us from becoming new—like jealously, lying, unforgiveness, wrong motives, ungodly thoughts, addictions, and other plans or deeds contrary to God's best for us. Often God allows circumstances or brings people into our lives to aid in the cutting process. "As iron sharpens iron, so one man sharpens another" (Proverbs 27:17). Our battles, conflicts, and confrontations are often used to show us our own faults and prompt us to allow God to take them out of our lives.

After the jug has been fashioned into a bird feeder, it is time to decorate it. Unlike the decorations of pictures, buttons, and pasta shells we put on the outside of the jug, the ornaments of the child of God should come from within. In 1 Peter 3:3–4, we are admonished, "Your beauty should not come from outward adornment, such as braided hair and the wearing of gold jewelry and fine clothes. Instead it should be that of your inner self, the unfading beauty of a gentle and quiet spirit, which is of great worth in God's sight." Of course, we must pay attention to personal hygiene, modest dress, and an attractive appearance, but these should not be our only concerns. Rather, living an exemplary life of love, righteousness, and wisdom is the model God uses as He makes us His vessels.

A Bird Feeder, Lord?

It is time to place our new bird feeder where it can be useful. First, we use twine to connect it to the branch. The connection is important because without it, the bird feeder will fall. Isn't that true in our walk with the Lord? "Abide in me, and I in you. As the branch cannot bear fruit of itself, except it abide in the vine; no more can ye, except ye abide in me" (John 15:4). We must stay connected to the Lord in order to be used in His service.

The final act in completing the bird feeder is filling it. Our Lord wants to fill us so we can be useful for His purpose. Just as putting marbles in the bird feeder would cause injury to the birds, so being filled with the wrong "food" will cause harm to those we wish to feed. Rather than trying to figure out what bad food is, let's just eat what Jesus eats. "Jesus saith unto them, My meat is to do the will of him that sent me, and to finish his work" (John 4:34).

Doing God's will fills us with all we need to nourish ourselves and be a benefit to others. It is God's will that we study His Word, pray, and obey Him. He has promised to fill us with His Spirit and equip us for His service. Just as the bird feeder serves a special purpose if it is properly filled, so we, as instruments of the Lord's work, will be vessels of honor for Him.

"For we are his workmanship, created in Christ Jesus unto good works, which God hath before ordained that we should walk in them" (Ephesians 2:10).

CHAPTER 9

Take Out the Garbage

One day, as I drove though the familiar neighborhoods on my way to work, I noticed discarded items along the sides of the road. Garbage bags, trash cans, old bikes, furniture, and cartons, each with its place in line along the tree lawns. There was no secret regarding what day it was—garbage day.

It was apparent that all the residents participated in garbage day. For at least one day per week, there was unity of purpose in the neighborhood. Of course, the consequences of non-compliance would be severe—respond on garbage day or be stuck with the stinky stuff for another whole week.

As I passed the refuse that had been expelled from the homes, I thought how refreshing it would be to have my own garbage day—the internal kind—to take the trash out of my life.

We don't have to wonder what might happen if we never took the garbage out of our homes. Imagine the vermin, disease, decay, and smell. Likewise, if we allow unclean or unsafe debris to pile up in our lives, our own existence will exude a similar odor.

The garbage of life is a combination of all the waste products of daily living, substances that are not useful to us. The garbage that tends to accumulate in our lives may include the following:

1. Sickness—a by-product of living in a world tainted by sin. It can show itself physically, mentally, or emotionally, and always impacts others around us. Long-term, sickness can further degrade into hopelessness.

2. Pain—a by-product of dealing with other people. Negative attitudes, conflicts, confrontations, and broken relationships can eventually wear down the natural gravitation we have toward other people. Pain, unchecked, can decay into bitterness.

3. Fear—a by-product of real and perceived dangers around us. Born out of the unknown, fear can cause us to build walls around ourselves to avoid contact with the feared people or situations. It can also perpetuate attacks against others, with a "strike first" attitude. In its most putrid condition, fear becomes jealousy, contempt, and hatred.

4. Doubt—a by-product of an accumulation of disappointments. Failure to pray, praying against God's will, or unwillingness to wait on the answer will result in our not receiving what we want. If we are not grounded in God's Word, we won't know how to biblically apply our faith and receive from God. Doubt thrives when we don't have a strong relationship with God, and we mistakenly attribute our disappointment

to some error or failure on God's part. As doubt festers, it becomes despair.

5. Worry—a by-product of instability. This world is full of uncertainties: wars, the economy, crime, natural disasters, and a myriad of other potential catastrophes. Among our responsibilities of work, school, family, church, and community, opportunities for worry are infinite. Aside from the physical damage worry causes, such as high blood pressure, ulcers, sleep disorders, etc., the person who worries feels overwhelmingly helpless. Worry, in its foulest state, becomes depression.

The waste materials from daily life can become part of our character if it is not periodically removed. We must expel from our lives the residue from the world or the stench of it will overcome the sweet aroma that was once ours when we were made new by Christ.

How do we take the garbage out? The formula is found in 1 Peter 5:7, "Casting all you cares upon him; for he careth for you" (KJV). Jesus wants to receive all the trash from our lives. He already paid for it with His blood, and He does not want us to carry it. God's Word is clear about how we are to empty ourselves of this world's garbage:

1. Sickness—Isaiah 53:5: "But he was wounded for our transgressions, he was bruised for our iniquities: the chastisement of our peace was upon him; and with his stripes we are healed."

2. Pain—Psalm 34:18–19: "The Lord is nigh unto them that are of a broken heart; and saveth such as be of a

contrite spirit. Many are the afflictions of the righteous: but the Lord delivereth him out of them all."

3. Fear—Psalm 118:5–6: "I called upon the Lord in distress: the Lord answered me and set me in a large place. The Lord is on my side; I will not fear: what can man do unto me?"

4. Doubt—Mark 11:23: "For verily I say unto you, that whosoever shall say unto this mountain, Be thou removed, and be thou cast into the sea; and shall not doubt in his heart, but shall believe that those things which he saith shall come to pass; he shall have whatsoever he saith."

5. Worry—Psalm 37:3–5: "Trust in the Lord, and do good; so shalt thou dwell in the land, and verily thou shalt be fed. Delight thyself also in the Lord; and he shall give thee the desires of thine heart. Commit thy way unto the Lord; trust also in him; and he shall bring it to pass."

Let us allow Jesus to take the garbage out of our lives. He wants to replace it with the freshness of His Spirit. Instead of permitting the trash of the world's ideas and attitudes to clutter our understanding, let's unload the hindrances through prayer. Then we can adorn ourselves with hope, peace, love, health, and the joy that comes only with a relationship with the clean, pure, holy God through Jesus Christ.

CHAPTER 10

"Don't Be No Punk"

Have you ever felt beaten down, bullied, attacked, or targeted? We all have at some time. We have an enemy, a bully. "The thief cometh not, but for to steal, and to kill, and to destroy . . . ." (John 10:10a). Our enemy lives to bully us, and he'll use people, circumstances, and even our own thoughts to do it.

My son experienced the ravages of our neighborhood bully. He spent months running, hiding, and taking all available measures to avoid confrontation with the (slightly) bigger boy. He would not defend himself for fear of being pulverized by the brute. About the tenth time my son came running home for shelter from the bully, his father stepped in. Despite my inclination to go have a "nice little talk" with the boy's mother, I submitted to my husband's solution. He said to my son, "Don't be no punk!" He went on to express that if he doesn't stand up to the bully now, he will always be running. I slipped in the comment that we'll be there for him if the boy's parents get involved—essentially, "We've got your back." My husband added the clincher, "If you ever again run instead of defending yourself, you'll have to deal with me!" Needless to say, my son did defend himself, won the battle, and as I am writing this, the two boys are playing peacefully together.

Perhaps not in the exact wording, but God is telling His children what my husband told our son, "Don't be no punk!" In 2 Timothy 1:7, we are told, "For God hath not given us the spirit of fear; but of power, and of love, and of a sound mind."

More than 40 times in Scripture, God says, "Fear not." He's telling us He's got our backs. "Fear not: for I am with thee . . ." (Isaiah 43:5a).

What does it mean to not be a punk? **Don't fall into self-pity.** Joseph was sold into slavery by his own brothers. His Egyptian masters had him unjustly imprisoned (Genesis 37–50). This series of events could have plunged Joseph into self-pity and depression. Instead, Joseph, determined to trust obediently in God, allowed God to use him. Joseph was eventually elevated to the second position in the kingdom, and God used him to save the entire region, including his family. What the enemy had meant to destroy Joseph, God turned to good (Genesis 50:20). Romans 8:28 tells us that all things work together for our good. And Romans 8:37 reminds us that we are more than conquerors through Christ. So we can't wallow in self-pity. Rather than feeling sorry for ourselves, we must know who we are and *whose* we are!

Don't lose hope. The opposite of hope is despair. Sometimes our fears and problems cause us to see no way out. In despair, we don't even try any more. In John 16:33, Jesus encourages us, "These things I have spoken unto you, that in me ye might have peace. In the world ye shall have tribulation: but be of good cheer; I have overcome the world." Our hope is in knowing that our God will cause us to be victorious. "Five of you shall chase a hundred, and a hundred of you shall put ten thousand to flight" (Leviticus 26:8, NKJV). As we remember God's promises, our hope will be strengthened. Even in difficult circumstances, hope keeps us pressing on. "But if we hope for that we see not, then do we with patience wait for it" (Romans 8:25).

Don't run. Sometimes we panic and run. We seek protection everywhere but with the Lord—courts, psychics, the lottery, alcohol, drugs, people. But Psalm 121:1–2 clearly tells us where to go when the bullying starts. "I will lift up mine eyes unto the hills, from whence cometh my help. My help cometh from the Lord, which made heaven and earth."

Okay. Now we know not to have self-pity, not to lose hope, and not to run. So, what *do* we do when the enemy causes us trouble? **Stand.** Ephesians, Chapter 6, outlines the protection God gives us as we stand—a shield (faith), a helmet (salvation), shoes (peace), a belt (truth), and a breastplate (righteousness). We only need one weapon—the sword of the Spirit, the Word of God. Notice in Ephesians 6:16–17, the enemy throws fiery darts, but we have a sword! In battle, which would you rather have, darts or a sword? God clearly shows us here who will win.

Once I had a dream that I was in a big yard with many of my family members and friends. We all had shields and swords. We were all shielding ourselves against flaming arrows that were flying through the air all around us. I was seized with fear, threw down my weapon, and started running away from the fight. Suddenly a hot piercing pain shot into my back (a fiery dart). Although this was a dream, I felt the sensation of a puncture for several minutes after I woke up. The Lord spoke to me through that dream, which He confirms in Ephesians 6. Notice that God doesn't mention back protection. Two reasons are apparent—we are never to turn around (Luke 9:62), and God's got our backs (Matthew 28:20).

In Exodus 14:13, Moses and the nation of Israel were up against certain annihilation at the Red Sea by the approaching Egyptian army. But Moses, through God's guidance, lifted his staff and said, "Stand and see the salvation of the Lord." Through miraculous events, Israel was saved and the enemy was completely destroyed! ". . . and having done all, to stand" (Ephesians 6:13).

Get in close. Have you ever watched what a toddler will do when he or she senses danger? That child will grab the parent's leg with a two-armed bear hug and won't let go. I picture God's children similarly responding as we grasp on to Him to protect us.

"Submit yourselves therefore to God. Resist the devil and he will flee from you. Draw nigh to God and he will draw nigh to you . . ." (James 4:7–8). First, you must resist the devil who is trying to steal your soul. Accept Jesus' perfect sacrifice for your sins. Ask Him to forgive you and come into your life and be your Savior and Lord. Talk to Him daily in prayer, listen to Him through His Word. Fellowship with other believers. Grow closer to God as you meditate on His promises. Then you can say with confidence, "If God be for me, who can be against me" (Romans 8:31).

Make the enemy run. We've read in James 4:7 that we can make the enemy run from us. Lest we get cocky and think we can accomplish this under our own power, let's recall what Jesus has told us in John 15:5, that without Him we can do nothing. However, Jesus gives us examples in Matthew 4, verses 4, 7, and 10. Each time Satan approached Jesus with a temptation, He responded with, "It is written . . . ." Each time, the Word was used to beat back the devil, and eventually he had to leave. If Jesus had to rely on the power of the Word, how much more should we? To defeat the bully, we need to speak the Word, study it, and know it. Then we can see victory, not defeat, out of our circumstances. ". . . The words that I speak unto you, they are spirit, and they are life" (John 6:63b).

So, don't be no punk. Don't fear, don't lose hope, and don't run. Stand, get close to God through Jesus Christ, and use your sword, the Word of God, to make the bully run. Now, let's finish the statement Jesus made in John 10:10, "The thief cometh not but for to steal, and to kill, and to destroy: I am come that they might have life, and that they might have it more abundantly."

LIKE A CHILD

Have you ever watched a child
At play, so light and free?
Without a care he gives his all
And scrambles fearlessly.

He runs his race with all his heart,
He knows that he can win.
And if he falls he jumps right up
And scampers off again.

He leaps with joy, he screams with glee,
His face lights up so bright,
To have his turn to play the game
Has brought him great delight.

He loves his team, obeys his coach,
And follows all the rules
So he can always do his best.
He never wants to lose.

That child is our example
Of how to live this life.
To cast our cares upon the Lord,
To walk in peace, not strife.

And may we, like that child, rejoice
In all the work we do.
And if we fail, may we confess
And let God make us new.

And let us love our brothers
And never cease to pray,
So when it comes our turn to share
We have the words to say.

"Don't Be No Punk"

Let's always know we're winners
And spread God's love around.
Let joy prevail within our hearts
And childlike faith abound.

PART III

Surrender in Worship

CHAPTER 11

Good Is Not Good Enough

"You did a good job on your homework." "The baby was good." "This pizza is good." "Boy, was that a good game!" "This has been a very good day." We use the word "good" to describe a vast array of people, places, things, and events. Generally, we agree on the meaning of the word as it appears in various contexts. As I think about this, I recall how many times I say, "God is good." Although God knows what I am attempting to communicate and the depths of the praise I am trying to voice, somehow the word "good" sounds almost mediocre when used to describe such an awesome being. Think about it—in one house a drug addict may be mumbling, "This heroin is good," while next door a saint may be shouting, "God is good!" No, to describe God, "good" just isn't good enough.

To find accurate adjectives to help us describe God, we might search the thesaurus. We would find synonyms for "good" such as fantastic, excellent, superb, superior, terrific, or flawless. But I decided to scan the Scriptures to find suitable terms to describe our Creator.

How does the Lord describe Himself? "I am the God that healeth thee" (Exodus 15:26). "I am the door" (John 10:9). "I am the Alpha and Omega, the beginning and the end, the first and the last" (Revelations 22:13). I am the way, the truth, and the life" (John 14:6). I am the light of the world" (John 8:12). "I am the bread of life" (John 6:48). "I am the vine" (John 15:5). "I am He that liveth, and was dead; and behold, I am alive for evermore" (Revelation 1:18). God uses these and dozens of other references to give us a guide to Who He is, and how we should describe Him in our praise.

In searching the Scriptures, we find that the ancient scribes recorded hundreds of descriptions of God. Isaiah refers to Him as Wonderful, Counselor, the Mighty God, the Everlasting Father, the Prince of Peace (Isaiah 9:6). Throughout the Psalms, David attributes such terms as: refuge, fortress, help, keeper, strong tower, deliverer, the King of Glory. Abraham knew God as provider (Genesis 22:8). After safely crossing the Red Sea, Moses and the Israelites proclaimed God as "my strength, my song, and he has become my salvation" (Exodus 15:2).

John calls Him the Word (John 1:1). Peter identifies Him as the Christ, the Son of the living God (Matthew 16:16). Paul describes Him as faithful (1 Corinthians 10:13). Jude recognizes that He is the only wise God our Savior (Jude 25). No matter how you slice it, God is much more than good.

Our Father is not such a stickler on semantics as to condemn us for using the same word to describe Him as we would to describe a pizza. No, He knows the thoughts and intents of our hearts and is pleased to hear us send forth genuine praises to Him. So, saying "God is good" is always appropriate. However, let us also pattern our praises after the many examples we have in God's Word. Let us lift up our voices and proclaim that God is love, mercy, truth, power, forgiving, all-knowing, Creator, Lord, King, etc., etc., etc. God is good!

CHAPTER 12

Downtime

Downtime. Oh, what a marvelous thought! A temporary oasis from the tedium or monotony of work; a moment of sanity to escape our frantic surroundings. We deserve it, don't we? Many of us feel guilty when we break from our rigors and relax. We fail to recognize that rest is an essential ingredient in a healthy, productive life. God himself introduced this concept in Genesis 2:2 when He rested from His work of creation. So if God rested, how much more do we, fragile beings that we are, need downtime?

The trouble with downtime is that it often becomes wasted time. What could become reflective, creative time is often stolen from us by the television or the couch. In too many cases, downtime becomes "lights out" for the brain, the body, and, sadly, the heart.

The perfect pattern for downtime is recorded in God's Word. In His guidelines for the Sabbath, God directs His people in the specific downtime activities that will be most beneficial for them. In Deuteronomy 5:12–15, we find the dictates—no working for sons, daughters, servants, oxen, mules, cattle, or visitors. Sabbath rules also included no buying, no selling, no locating property, or trying out beasts of burden. Did that mean God intended for His people to vegetate every Saturday? Hardly. From the first mention of the Jewish Sabbath in Exodus 16:23 to the Christians' first day of the week commemoration of Jesus rising from the dead in Matthew 28:1, the establishment of a special day of rest is based on the same command—*give the day to the Lord*. He wants us to place ourselves in His presence through praise, to concentrate on His greatness in our worship, to meditate on His Word, and to bring Him glory through our conversations.

If God's people devote one day per week solely to God, think how He will speak to us! We will rise out of a day in His presence with profound revelation that is only found around the Throne. And this is not a practical impossibility. Those saints who have surrendered all to the Lord are already doing this on a daily basis. In our fellowship, at our meals, in our play, on our vacations, keep this thought: Remember the downtime and keep it holy.

CHAPTER 13

Talk To the Hand!

One day I was watching a talk show on television. The discussion involved parents who could not control their young teen and pre-teen children. I stared incredulously as children verbally assaulted their tearful parents. One ten-year-old, whose mother was attempting to correct her, put her hand up in front of her mother's face and retorted, "Talk to the hand!"

I was shocked at the disrespect and defiance those youngsters showed their parents, but I thought about that rebellious little girl's use of this popular insult, "Talk to the hand." It made me think about the hand. What about the hand? The hand has multiple purposes:

1) Doing daily routines (brushing teeth, eating, zipping, buttoning, combing hair)
2) Providing (cooking, cleaning, fixing, feeding)
3) Nurturing (patting, holding, comforting)
4) Healing (giving medicine, bandaging, massaging)
5) Communicating (receiving, giving, gesturing, waving)

God made our hands to perform a variety of tasks. Genesis 1:26–27 reminds us that He has made us in His image, so it makes sense to believe that His hands can do an infinite number of tasks. Let's take a moment to ponder what it means to "talk to the hand." Not our hands, but the hand of the Almighty God.

The hand of God is often described as a hand of vengeance. True, judgment will indeed come upon those who have worked against God's purpose and His people. Hebrews 10:31 (KJV) warns us, "It is a fearful thing to fall into the hands of the living God." God is not playing with us. He does not tolerate rebellion and sin, and He will exact justice to the ungodly. However, God is often characterized *only* by this attribute and, consequently, many people are afraid of Him. But God also has a hand we *can* talk to, capable of addressing every need that concerns us.

"Fear not, for I am with you; be not dismayed, for I am your God. I will strengthen you, yes, I will help you, I will uphold you with my righteous right hand" (Isaiah 41:10, NKJV). God upholds us—that means He *supports* us when we are down. Picture yourself walking on an icy surface and beginning to slip. The first instinctive motion is for your hands to reach out for support. Spiritually, God's hand will do likewise—lift us up when we stumble, such as when we fall into temptation or sin. "Now unto Him who is able to keep us from falling . . ." (Jude 24a). St. Jude understood that God's loving hand will lend us the support we need during times of testing and weakness.

"My sheep hear my voice, and I know them and they follow me. And I give them eternal life; and they shall never perish; neither shall anyone snatch them out of my hand. My Father, who has given them to me, is greater than all; and no one is able to snatch them out of my Father's hand. I and my Father are one" (John 10:27–30, NKJV). Jesus, God the Son, gives us an example of God's hand of *protection*. By trusting in Jesus as Savior and Lord, we shall be eternally with God; no one can take us out of His hand.

How does God use His hands? Genesis describes how God created all things. He spoke light into existence (Genesis 1:3). He spoke, and sea and dry land were created (Genesis 1:9). God, by speaking, brought all plant life into being (Genesis 1:11–12). With a word, God created the sun, moon, and stars (Genesis 1:14–18). Then by merely speaking, He made all manner of animal life (Genesis 1:20–25). The entire universe He created by His Word alone. But, as we are shown in Genesis 2:7, God used His *hands* to create man from the dust of the ground! He used a *personal touch* to create us. He demonstrated at creation that He takes a special interest in humankind.

A touch makes any encounter closer. Whether comforting, assisting, advising, or listening, physical contact (a pat on the shoulder, a touch on the hand, a hug, etc.) makes our involvement much more personal. Isaiah 64:8 (NKJV) tells us "But now, O Lord, You are our Father; we are the clay and You our Potter, and all we are the work of Your hand." God's unlimited love towards us is exhibited in the fact that He took the time to form us with His very own hands.

Jesus, God the Son, used His hands to heal, to save, and to do miracles. The Matthew 8:3 account of the healing of the man with leprosy is one of countless records of healings done by Jesus. In Matthew 14:25–31, we read about Jesus rescuing Peter out of the sea after his brief experience walking on water. From two fish and five loaves of bread, Jesus showed the miraculous work of His hand in feeding more than 5,000 people (Matthew 14:14–21). Jesus is still healing, saving, and doing miracles by His hand today!

When Jesus became the sacrifice for our sins, even from the cross, He gave us an example of His powerful hand. He was nailed to the cross by His feet, which signifies that He had gone everywhere He needed to go to establish His church in the world. His hands also were nailed to the cross, depicting that He had done everything necessary to provide all we would ever need. In essence, Jesus' hands and feet had performed their mission on this earth. In John 19:30, Jesus said, "It is finished," which punctuated His work in human flesh.

"Surely he has borne our griefs and carried our sorrows; yet we esteemed him stricken, smitten by God and afflicted. But he was wounded for our transgressions, he was bruised for our iniquities; the chastisement for our peace was upon him, and by his stripes we are healed" (Isaiah 53:4–5, NKJV). The sacrifice of Jesus has given us access to all we shall ever need. Jesus is telling us essentially, "I have already made the medicine, you come and get it. I have prepared the meal, you come and eat it. I have wrapped the gift, you just receive it!" And when He rose from the dead, Jesus said in Matthew 28:18, "All power is given unto me in heaven and in earth." So, when we talk to the Lord in prayer, we are talking to the all-powerful hand that:

heals
provides
does miracles
saves
supports
feeds us
and defends us.

Whatever our needs are, we should talk to the Hand, the Mighty Hand of the Living God!

CHAPTER 14

Assume a Position

Part 1

"Stand still and see the salvation of the Lord . . ." (Exodus 14:13). "Having done all, to stand" (Ephesians 6:13). "Stand fast in the Lord" (Philippians 4:1). "Stand fast in faith" (2 Corinthians 1:24). "Stand praying" (Mark 11:25).

God often compels His people through Scripture to stand. Stand. What's so special about that particular posture that it appears so many times on God's command list? In order to find the significance of this commission, let's first find its definition:

>   Stand—1) to keep an upright position. He can *stand* upon his feet.
>   2) to remain valid, unchanged. The jury's verdict will *stand*.
>   3) to resist or endure. The house will *stand* through the storm.

To stand *upright* in the spiritual sense means to be righteous. Now we can be assured that in acknowledging God's call for us to stand, He does not intend for us to stand in our own righteousness. In fact, the Bible clearly states about mankind, "As it is written, there is none righteous, no, not one" (Romans 3:10). God declares in Isaiah 64:6 that our brand of righteousness is as filthy rags—not dusty, not soiled, but *filthy*; not cleansable, fit only to be thrown away. No, God has provided His righteousness, and has made it available through Jesus Christ. Jesus himself tells us to hunger and thirst after His righteousness (Matthew 6:33). To stand upright is to make decisions that are pleasing to God. The wisdom to make such decisions comes from knowing Him. James 1:5 reveals to us that the Father will liberally give us wisdom if we ask. God wants us to prosper, and to do so, we must choose His way, through His righteousness.

To stand *valid* means unchanged, standing on a base that will not move. Jesus' parable of the houses in Matthew 7:24–25 exemplifies the importance of building our lives upon an unshakeable foundation. We must be grounded in Jesus, the Rock, unwavering in our faith (James 1:6–8). The apostle Paul admonishes us in 1 Corinthians 15:58 (KJV) that we are to be "steadfast, unmovable, always abounding in the work of the Lord."

To stand *resisting* means to withstand or endure without being destroyed. Imagine flame-resistant or water-resistant clothing. It does not stop the fire or water from coming, but the clothing will not be destroyed by it. Likewise, as we stand resistant to the temptations of the world, the flesh, and the devil, we won't fall into ruin. Do we stand unprotected? Of course not. Ephesians 6 tells us about the armor we have at our disposal while we are standing. The armor for spiritual warfare is available to each believer. The writer introduces this protective covering with "Having done all, to stand."

The power by which we stand, however, does not come from ourselves. The Spirit of God lives in the body of each believer, which He calls "the temple" (1 Corinthians 6:19), and He supplies the power that enables us to stand.

"But we have this treasure in earthen vessels that the excellency of the power may be of God, and not of us" (2 Corinthians 4:7). Paul further predicts our victory in Romans 8:37 (NKJV), "Yet in all these things we are more than conquerors through Him who loved us."

Part 2

Are there times when we can't stand? Undoubtedly, we all experience times of frailty, infirmity, or weariness, when we can only *lean* on the Lord. In John 13:23, and a number of other gospel passages, we see John, "the disciple whom Jesus loved" leaning on His breast. John's display of affection meant that he put his trust in Jesus for the wisdom of His words, the power of His presence, and the protection found in closeness to Him.

When we find ourselves in extreme need to receive from God, we often *kneel* before Him. Humility, the acknowledgment of the unchallengeable sovereignty of God, is often characterized by the act of kneeling. The leper, in Mark 1:40, as he petitioned Jesus to heal him, knelt in complete surrender to His worthiness. The man's body language indicated that he was helpless, without hope, and that only the merciful hand of Jesus could change his circumstances. Just as Jesus' answer was "I will" to that leper's request, so our loving Lord will extend His compassion to all who sincerely and in faith kneel before Him.

Ezekiel displayed the ultimate show of humility in Ezekiel 3:23–24. He found himself in the glorious presence of the King of Kings, and his response—to fall on his face. What else could he do? At that moment, he recognized the nothingness of mankind compared to the omnipotent majesty of the Almighty God. It amuses me when I hear Christians rehearse all the questions and comments they plan to recite to Jesus when they get to heaven. My guess is that they will all be doing what I'll be doing—lying prostrate before the Lord, *face-down* and speechless! Isaiah, when confronted with God's infinite sovereignty and holiness, could only utter, "Woe is me! For I am undone; because I am a man of unclean lips, and I dwell in the midst of a people of unclean lips: for mine eyes have seen the King, the Lord of Hosts" (Isaiah 6:5). We, too, when we follow deeply into the presence of God through worship of Him, can begin to realize the awesome greatness only He possesses. Those are the times we, like Ezekiel, will fall prostrate at His feet.

No matter what positions we use to express our love and dependence on God, all revolve around Him through our Lord Jesus Christ. Whether we stand, we stand by His power; if we lean, we lean on Him for security and rest. As we kneel, we kneel to His sovereignty and compassion; in our lying prostrate before Him, we do so as recognition of His majestic holiness.

Assume a position. Acknowledge God for who He is—the God who created all things for His glory.

> "For from Him and through Him and to Him are all things. For all things originate with Him and come from Him; all things live through Him, and all things center in and tend to consummate and to end in Him. To Him be glory forever! Amen—so be it."
>
> (Romans 11:36, AMP)

CHAPTER 15

God's Presents or God's Presence?

"In Thy presence is fullness of joy . . . ."

(Psalm 16:11)

As a parent, I recall many times coming home and my children meeting me at the door. I've learned to expect one of two responses from them; either, "Mommy, you're home!" or "What did you bring me?" Of these two, which do you think gives me more joy? You guessed it! Like most parents, I want to hear that my boys are glad to see me before they start asking what I brought them. God feels exactly the same way. He wants His children to seek His presence, not just His presents.

Presents are gifts. God wants to bless His children, and He enjoys giving gifts. In Matthew 7:11, Jesus tells us, "If ye then, being evil, know how to give good gifts unto your children, how much more shall your Father which is in heaven give good things to them that ask him?" It gives God pleasure to give us gifts—His presents, but He more enjoys it when we want to seek His face—His presence.

Solomon, King David's son, had newly acquired the throne of Israel. One night in a dream, the Lord came to him and said, "Ask what I shall give thee" (1 Kings 3:5). God was offering Solomon a blank check for anything his heart desired. Had I been in Solomon's shoes, I would have tried my best to break the bank! But the Scriptures describe Solomon's response as quite different than mine would have been. Solomon thought about the great nation he was responsible to lead, the complex needs of the people, and the awesome task of protecting God's people from their many enemies. Solomon's request, as recorded in 1 Kings 3:9 was, "Give therefore thy servant an understanding heart to judge Thy people, that I may discern between good and bad." Solomon asked the Lord for His wisdom. This so pleased God that He gave Solomon wisdom above any man who had ever been born or would ever live. To this day, we equate King Solomon with his wisdom. In addition, 1 Kings 3:13 reveals that God gave more than Solomon asked. "And I have also given thee that which thou has not asked, both riches and honor so that there shall not be any among the kings like unto thee in all thy days."

What a marvelous example for us to see the multiple benefits of seeking God and His attributes. Jesus tells us in Matthew 6:33 "But seek ye first the kingdom of God and His righteousness, and all these things will be added unto you."

When we seek God's presents without seeking His presence, we shortchange ourselves. True, everybody likes to receive presents. Presents make us happy. The word "happy" means feeling contented pleasure. This feeling is based on what happens to us. Good things happen—we're happy. Bad things happen—we're unhappy. In this world, as good and bad happen every day, to depend on happiness would throw even the best of us onto an emotional roller coaster. God wants much more for us. He doesn't want us to be merely happy, which is temporary. He wants us to have *joy*, which is eternal. Joy is not dependent upon what happens, but on the assurance that God is with us, ordering our steps.

"In thy presence is fullness of joy." The presence of God means God is with us. God promises, "I will never leave you nor forsake you" (Hebrews 13:5). So the joy doesn't come when God is present, but joy comes when we *realize* that God is present. When we recognize His presence in every circumstance and are aware of His presence, even when our minds tell us we are all alone, then joy is released in our spirits.

There are obstacles to enjoying the presence of God. Sin cuts off our awareness of God. After we've sinned, we're often afraid or ashamed to approach Him. But God says to us, "If we confess our sins, he is faithful and just to forgive us our sins and to cleanse us from all unrighteousness" (1 John 1:9). God is eager to restore fellowship with His children when we admit our sins and allow His Spirit to cleanse and renew us. We can again be welcomed into His presence and experience the joy of His goodness.

The distractions of life can also be obstacles to enjoying the presence of God. There is a myriad of legitimate duties to be performed in the course of a day. As believers, we must put forth extra effort to make time and find a quiet place to commune with God. Jesus teaches us in Matthew 6:6 (NKJV), "But you, when you pray, go into your room, and when you have shut your door, pray to your Father who is in the secret place; and your Father who sees in secret will reward you openly."

Sometimes that secret place of prayer is hard to find. Daniel, when he was a captive of Babylon, found a place to pray in his house and did not fail to go there and fellowship with God three times a day, even when there was a law against it (Daniel 6). Even in the face of death, Daniel was faithful to pray. God rewarded him with divine deliverance from the lion's den. We should be diligent to overcome the distractions and make time in our day to pray.

Fear or unbelief can keep us from recognizing God's presence. Sometimes, particularly during our most difficult times, we may not be sure God is listening or that He even wants to hear from us. But God's Word tells us quite the opposite. "Let us therefore come boldly unto the throne of grace, that we may obtain mercy, and find grace to help in time of need" (Hebrews 4:16). God wants us to approach Him, just as parents want their children to come to them for the love, attention, and support they need.

How do we get into the presence of God? Praise! Psalm 22:3 tells us that God inhabits the praises of His people. Praise is reminding God who He is—not as though He needs reminding, but *we* need reminding. This is not thanksgiving for what God does for us (although we are also thankful), but praise is acknowledging who He *is*. He is all powerful, all knowing, healer, provider, sovereign . . . . He deserves praise for His strength, mercy, forgiveness, love, grace . . . . When we enter into His presence through praising Him, we put ourselves in a position to receive "joy unspeakable and full of glory."

"Where the Spirit of the Lord is there is liberty." (2 Corinthians 3:17, NKJV). Living in God's presence allows us the freedom to walk in the destiny He has chosen for us. That also includes the presents—the gifts of the Spirit and the abundant life that only come through relationship with God through Jesus Christ.

Live a joy-filled life. Seek God's presence, and the presents will come.

IF GOD WOULD ANSWER "WHY"

In all my painful moments
I never understood
How God in His omnipotence
Was working for my good.

I begged Him for the reasons
To all my many "whys."
"My thoughts are not your thoughts," He says,
And dries my weary eyes.

But what if God would answer?
Imagine what He'd say
To all my cries of "Why, Lord, why?"
What words would He convey?

Lord, why when I was sick so long
You didn't hear my prayer?
I heard, my child, and spared your life,
And taught you how to care.

And Lord, the time I lost my job
And things were getting worse.
You had to lose your livelihood
To find that I'm your Source.

Why did you take my loved ones
And leave me all alone?
To end their pain, complete their joy,
So they can welcome you home.

When enemies harassed me
Lord, I couldn't hear your voice.
I taught you how to meditate,
And through it all rejoice.

Dialogue with the Master

Forgive me Lord for doubting you
And thank you for your love.
For all good things have come from you,
You send them from above.

You're frail, my child, I understand.
But this you must recall,
My Spirit lives within your heart,
I'll never let you fall.

PART IV

Living the Good Life

CHAPTER 16

Remote Control God

Isn't the remote control a wonderful gadget? You turn on the television, switch channels, and avoid commercials, all without going near the TV. Now, to date myself a little, I remember the old black and white set with the dial. At our house, whichever of us kids was in the room at the time, received the mandate from Dad to turn the channel. By today's standards, that was quite a primitive undertaking. We had to walk across the room, turn the dial (although most of the time the dial was gone and we had to use pliers), and turn to Dad's choice of the three channels we received. Oh, I won't talk about adjusting the antennae on top with the fork stuck in the middle and the tin foil on the rabbit ears for reception! Anyway, right when I thought it couldn't get any better than our first color console, somebody invented the ingenious remote control.

The remote is a beloved instrument, cherished by boys and men alike. The remote teaches us that we can have what we want when we want it with little or no effort. Modern conveniences such as the remote can simplify our lives, but in our comfort, we can become lazy. Complacency can be dangerous if it creeps into other areas of our lives, particularly our spiritual lives.

God is not a remote control God. There are no buttons to push or special combinations that will make Him change His mind on the way He chooses to deal with us. We can't skip what we don't like or only choose what we enjoy. Unlike using the remote, we cannot stand far from God and expect Him to respond to our transmissions. No, God has standards and procedures outlined in His Word. Only those who obey His commands can expect to receive from Him. Remember, we serve God; He does not serve us. Ananias and Sapphira discovered this in Acts 5:1–11. They thought God would lower His standards of integrity and devotion. They held money back from their offering and falsely stated that they had sold their land and given all they had to the Lord. Both were given an immediate death sentence on the grounds that they had lied to the Holy Ghost.

Jonah found that no amount of "fiddling with the buttons" would change the assignment God had given him. The book of Jonah tells how the prophet was commanded to go preach in Nineveh, an exceedingly wicked city. After attempting to talk God out of it, Jonah tried to switch channels, traveling by ship in the opposite direction of Nineveh. After being thrown off the ship and spending three days inside the belly of a huge fish, Jonah finally figured out that God would not be controlled.

Jesus realized that His Father's will was preeminent over His own in Luke 22:42 (NKJV). He was about to go to the cross, and as He agonized in prayer, He said, "Father, if it is your will take this cup away from me, nevertheless not my will, but yours be done." He realized that God the Father had sent Him to save the world, and the instrument He would use would be the cross of Calvary.

God is sovereign. In Hebrew, He is called "El Elyon," the Lord Most High. No matter what social current, lifestyle, or political mood sweeps our society, God is still God, and His standards do not change. What was sin in ancient times is still sin today. The Ten Commandments that were delivered through Moses are still to be obeyed today. We cannot outsmart or hide from God. He is not moved by our attempts to justify our refusal to obey Him.

"For my thoughts are not your thoughts, nor your ways my ways," says the Lord. For as the heavens are higher than the earth, so are my ways higher than your ways, and my thoughts than your thoughts" (Isaiah 55:8–9, NKJV). We should rejoice when our attempts to manipulate God fail. God has wonderful things for us to experience if we are patient and obedient.

God is not a remote control God. Don't try to press His buttons or change His will. Go with the flow; stick with the program; follow God's plan. He sees the big picture and knows what is best for us. "For I know the thoughts that I think toward you, says the Lord, thoughts of peace and not of evil, to give you a future and a hope" (Jeremiah 29:11, NKJV).

CHAPTER 17

Bear, Just Bear

In my back yard stands a lone pear tree. It's probably a century old, and we expect it to find its rest in the neighbor's yard come the next windstorm. It is by far the least attractive tree I've ever seen. Because of its odd configuration of twisted branches, it does not provide shade. While I'm complaining about this decrepit tree, let me add that I'm not at all fond of its pears, either. Even with my unspoken desire to see that tree blown down and carted away, I am obliged to admit that this eyesore has several commendable qualities.

Every year, without fail, this tree bears fruit. The first to bud in the spring, this old tree withstands the late-March winds and snows without bowing to the last of winter's persistent bellows. With ceaseless resilience, this tree repairs itself and regrows buds that are determined to burst into gentle white blossoms and, ultimately, fruit.

As I watch the transformation of this tree from its winter's nakedness through to its autumn bounty, I notice one perennial constant. The tree does not move from its place. It never tries to relocate to a sunnier spot or a more comfortable climate. It doesn't try to push other trees aside. Neither does my tree try to dress itself with another tree's leaves. The birds and insects always know where to find refuge and nourishment. The deer and geese can depend on my tree to provide a ready snack. Essentially, my tree stays put, rooting itself continuously deeper in its place, faithfully bearing fruit.

This ugly pear tree can teach us volumes about how we are to manage the Christian walk. As we grow in Christ, we should, like that tree, become rooted deeper and deeper in the Word of God. "Let the Word of Christ dwell in you richly in all wisdom" (Colossians 3:16). As God's Word opens our understanding to His will and His voice, we shall become more stable, resolved, and rooted in the things of God. "Be ye steadfast, unmovable, always abounding in the work of the Lord . . ." (1 Corinthians 15:58).

Although my tree bears fruit annually, I have never seen it reach into the soil looking for the ingredients to use. I have never viewed its branches mixing or kneading, molding or sculpturing the pears, or in any way striving to create its own fruit. It simply *is what it is*, a pear tree. And because it stays what it is, it naturally does what it does—bears pears. This observation exemplifies that God's people should likewise be what we are—new creations in Christ Jesus, filled with His Spirit, patiently bearing His fruit. "Abide in me, and I in you. As the branch cannot bear fruit of itself, except it abide in the vine; no more can ye, except ye abide in me" (John 15:4,). Jesus reminds us here that the Spirit of God supplies the fruit; our job is to yield to Him and allow Him to produce the fruit in us.

"But the fruit of the Spirit is love, joy, peace, longsuffering, kindness, goodness, faithfulness, gentleness, self-control. Against such there is no law" (Galatians 5:22–23, NKJV). It is a futile effort to create our own fruit. If we look around us, we can find an assortment of failed attempts at "fruit-making." For instance, the world has several self-created versions of love, ranging from approval to lust to control. The world's interpretation of joy involves temporal pleasures, most of which are dissatisfying and destructive. Peace is often sought in a bottle, a bank, or a prescription. Goodness and kindness are selfish and conditional. In present-day society, little attempt is made at even a counterfeit version of gentleness, patience, or self-control. No, we cannot—no matter how much energy we expend—create fruit that will be pleasing to God.

Bear, just bear. Let's strengthen our relationship with Jesus by talking to Him, obeying Him, studying His Word, and listening for the leading of the Holy Spirit in our lives. Let's keep our thoughts clean and our attitudes right. God is looking for "trees" to nourish and shelter those in need. Let's bear the fruit that will draw the hungry to us so that they may be fed and strengthened. "For the fruit of the Spirit is in all goodness and righteousness and truth" (Ephesians 5:9, NKJV).

CHAPTER 18

Wood, Hay, and Stubble

"Redeeming the time, for the days are evil. Wherefore be not unwise, but understanding what the will of the Lord is."
(Ephesians 5:16–17)

When the apostle Paul penned these words nearly two thousand years ago, his world was described as evil. How much more evil is it now that, in addition to the Ten Commandment-breaking sins that we've always had, we have new avenues for evil. Our modern technology has allowed us to add nuances to our sin. With video adultery and cyber theft, we can bear false witness on the superhighway and covet on credit. With temptation so prevalent around us, we are compelled to heed Paul's admonition to redeem (or use wisely) the time, for these days are truly evil.

We can recognize sin. We know the difference between right and wrong. God has made sure that we know because He has written His laws on our hearts (Romans 2:15). Therefore, we are without excuse. But the title here, "Wood, Hay, and

Stubble," does not refer to the devastation left by sin in the life of the ungodly. Wood, hay, and stubble refer to the kinds of work performed by the careless Christian.

According to the prophetic words in 1 Corinthians 3:11–15, when we who are saved stand before God in heaven, our works will be tried by fire. The works that remain are called "gold, silver, and precious stones," and those works that burn up are "wood, hay, and stubble." These are all "good works," but the motives and intentions of our hearts determine their value in the eyes of God. For instance, giving is a good work. If we give cheerfully, as instructed in 2 Corinthians 9:7, God is pleased. But given grudgingly, as this verse also describes, is not pleasing to God and will not withstand the trial by fire. Prayer is another good work. But if the motive is to be seen and heard by others, we are like the hypocrites Jesus referred to in Matthew 6:5, and wood, hay, and stubble will be our reward. Genuine prayer in secret, as Jesus instructed in Matthew 6:6, will yield gold, silver, and precious stones.

What about the church work we do? All church work is good, right? God's Word is quite specific on the work of the church. First, the final command from Jesus as He ascended from this earth was, "Go ye into all the world and preach the gospel to every creature" (Mark 16:15). The most prominent work of the church should be in response to this mandate. The salvation of souls must be the primary goal of church work if it is to be regarded as gold, silver, and precious stones. Secondly, we are to teach all nations (Matthew 28:18–20). That is, the church is to reach out to new Christians and help them grow in the faith. Preaching and teaching based on the Word of God are certainly good works that will remain, as long as we are careful to rightly divide the word of truth (2 Timothy 2:15).

Jesus predicted rewards for His "sheep" who humbly serve others in Matthew 25:31–40. Feeding, clothing, visiting, and comforting others are all good works when we do them in the name of Jesus and for His glory.

Those of us with a love for the Lord and the heart of a servant often become overwhelmed when we look at so many needs around us. We can burn out trying to do every job that needs to be done. God does not intend for this to happen. "Now ye are the body of Christ, and members in particular" (1 Corinthians 12:27). The writer further explains here that we all have different functions, but we are all necessary. God has a purpose and a place for each of us to work based on the talents He has given us and the steps He has ordered for us. As we perform the work God has called us to do, our service for the kingdom of God will be gold, silver, and precious stones.

There is wood, hay, and stubble created when we do works that are outside our calling. I learned this lesson personally several years ago. When I accepted Christ in 1981, I was a school teacher. Naturally, I assumed that my calling in the church should be teaching Sunday school and children's ministries. Within a few months in this area, I began to feel restless and frustrated. I started to dread Sunday mornings when it was my turn to lead. I didn't tell anyone how miserable I was because, after all, I was "working for the Lord." One day, as I was praying, God whispered to me the instructions He had for me. The next day I went out to the public square in the middle of town and began street witnessing. Since that day, nearly all the work I have done has been evangelistic, and my joy is to reach souls who have never heard the Good News. There is nothing wrong with Sunday school and children's ministries, but I was the wrong person for the job. And guess what? As soon as I got out of the way, God placed the people in those ministries He intended to be there, who, by the way, are thriving to this day.

We have all heard of preachers who have "called themselves" into the ministry—wood, hay, and stubble. Paul confirms this in Philippians 1:14–18 when he outlines the various motives people have for preaching the gospel.

Wouldn't it be a shame to work, work, work for the church for decades, only to have it all burned up when we get to heaven? How do we avoid ending up with wood, hay, and stubble? The first and easiest thing to do is to check our motives. Paul says in 2 Corinthians 13:5 (KJV), "Examine yourselves whether ye be in the faith . . . ." Let's ask ourselves a few questions:

1. Will I do this if no one notices me for it?
2. Will I feel hurt if no one thanks me?
3. Will I do this even if it isn't popular?
4. Will I quit if I'm not voted in as the leader?
5. Will I quit if things are not done my way?
6. Am I doing this just to show others that I can?

These are obviously not questions to be answered out loud, but it would be beneficial to meditate on our motives to see if they are pleasing to God.

Secondly, we must be sure we are within the will of God. Consider the gifts, talents, skills, and interests He has already given to us. Listen for His gentle leading as He guides us into the ministries He has for us. Allow Him to confirm the calling through His Word, His people, and the doors He will open in our lives.

Let's go for the gold. Let's seek God's perfect will for our lives. Let's use the talents we have received in service for Him. Let's check our attitudes and inventory our motives. Time is short; let's not waste it doing works that will be burned up. "For the Son of Man shall come in the glory of his Father with his angels; and then he shall reward every man according to his works" (Matthew 16:27).

CHAPTER 19

Grease the Wheels

"Stir up the gift of God which is in you."
(2 Timothy 1:6, NKJV)

On the third day of spring break, I decided that I had enjoyed enough rest and it was time to clean house. In a symbolic act of self-sacrifice, I trekked into the boys' bedroom. When I finally found the bunk beds, I noticed a virtual city of toys under the bottom bunk. At closer look, I recognized several toys that they had received just four months prior as Christmas presents—under the bed, collecting dust. All that money we spent, and they had lost interest already. My boys begged for months for these very toys. Their excitement on Christmas morning as they opened these gifts was unforgettable. And now, here they were, lying forgotten and neglected under the bed. I was deflated.

My frustration over how quickly my sons had lost their enthusiasm for their toys made me wonder if I had ever exasperated my Father like that. I had a flashback to the time I received my most cherished gift—salvation. Oh, the excitement! Oh, the zeal I had! I wanted everybody to be saved, and I was going to see to it that everyone would hear the message from me. I carried gospel tracts everywhere I went. I told store clerks, waiters, and gas station attendants that Jesus loved them. I received polite smiles, smirks, blank stares, and snarls; I didn't care—I loved Jesus!

As I grew in the Word, I began to understand the leading of the Spirit in my witnessing. I began to pray for opportunities to minister to hearts that were ready to receive. I gained wisdom on how to lead others to Christ and how to speak words seasoned with salt (Colossians 4:6). I bought witnessing tapes and books and attended evangelism classes. As my ability to minister was increasing, that childlike zeal was subtly decreasing. Although I hadn't seen it coming, I was becoming preoccupied with learning how to lead others to Christ, yet I was beginning to lose that infectious joy that had been drawing others to me. Ministry was becoming a job rather than the joyous privilege it had once been. I began to feel like a wagon with rusty wheels, trudging along its arduous route. I still loved the Lord, but my enthusiasm was waning. I needed to "grease the wheels" in my spiritual life so I could move along more smoothly on the path God had chosen for me.

How could I awaken from the sluggishness I had allowed to come over me? God's Word, our guide for life, has the answer. "Stir up the gift of God that is in you." In 2 Timothy 1:6 we are encouraged that God has placed gifts in us and admonished to not allow them to become dormant. In this passage, Timothy was a young preacher launching out into ministry. His mentor, the apostle Paul, was instructing him on how to fulfill his calling with the success God intended for him to have. It had been in his childhood that Timothy became aware that God had a plan for his life. Paul was reminding Timothy of the spiritual gifts God had placed in his life earlier, and admonishing him to stir them up. Timothy was being encouraged to allow the Holy Spirit to work the gifts to the surface so he could perform his ministry in power.

Stirring a dwindling fire can spark the embers, restart the fire, and produce the desired heat and light. At times we all need to be stirred up so our gifts can be brought up from their dormancy. To do this, we must seek God to awaken our ministry gifts (Romans 12:6–8) and our spiritual gifts (1 Corinthians 12:8–11). Let it be our prayer that God will revive the fire that had burned so brightly before.

In order to use the gifts God has given us, we must be loosed, lubricated, "greased" with oil. Throughout the Scriptures, oil has represented the Holy Spirit. When the prophet Samuel anointed David with oil (1 Samuel 16:13), it signified that God had chosen him to be king. The oil meant that the Holy Spirit was upon David to guide him through his reign. In Jesus' first sermon in the synagogue, He announced, "The Spirit of the Lord is upon me, because he hath anointed me to preach the gospel to the poor . . ." (Luke 4:18). Although Jesus is God, and possesses all power as He reigns in Heaven, when He came to earth in the form of man, He purposely limited himself to live as a human. Therefore, He relied, as we must, on the Holy Spirit to work through Him on earth. It is that same anointing Paul spoke of in James 5:14–15 when he instructed the sick to call for the elders, ". . . anointing him with oil in the name of the Lord."

It is God's desire to fill us with the Holy Spirit. As we seek His fullness, He will anoint us with His power, and our walk with Jesus will be energized. Let's begin to "grease the wheels" by stirring up the gifts within us and by receiving a fresh anointing with the oil of the Holy Spirit.

For You Who Helped Me Grow

For those who know you, it's no surprise
You're acknowledged, adored, and admired.
But I'd like to take time and announce to the world
How my life you've so richly inspired.

You are my mentor, my teacher, my dear loyal friend,
You've been there with support and advice.
Through the joking and laughing and talking and prayer,
Even scolding me good once or twice.

Sweet-spirited wisdom and comforting words
And your gentleness, soft as a dove,
How you listen, encourage, and never mislead.
You have been there with kindness and love.

As you helped me to grow you have opened the Word
Being careful to always be right.
From the day I came in from the darkness of sin
You've been pointing my way to the Light.

God's grace is upon you, His power within,
You're His vessel, I'm so glad you're here.
You're my mentor, my teacher, my God-given friend,
And I thank you for keeping me near.

Love,
Beverly

PART V

We Win!

CHAPTER 20

It's Not What You Know, It's Who You Know

In nearly every realm of earthly life there are those who, because of their birth or relationships, enjoy certain advantages the rest of us don't enjoy. Some get special privileges such as easy loans, property, or extra rights. Others use their influence to get out of trouble such as arrests, or paying penalties or taxes. We often see the privileged avoid responsibilities like working or military service. Indeed, in the world in which we live, the adage is true: It's not what you know; it's who you know.

I once had a job in which I watched others climb the ladder who I know were not as capable as I (in my opinion). I felt as though I just didn't have the connections I needed to get ahead. As I prayed, I felt the Lord showing me this statement slightly revised, "It's not what you know, it's Whom you know." I began to think a little differently. You see, I had forgotten whom I know, and how He would place me in a position of success. Psalm 46:10 (KJV) tells me, "Be still and know that I am God: I will be exalted among the heathen, I will be exalted in the earth."

This made me think about what it means to know God. The word "know" means: 1) to notice, 2) to identify, 3) to recognize, 4) to have a relationship with, 5) to become intimate with, and 6) to unite with.

To notice. Look around outside on a bright, beautiful day. Observe nature—the trees, the bountiful colors that never clash, the animals as they stay true to their instincts, the miracle of life that has been constant since God first spoke it into being. The timeless balance of nature causes us to know there is a God. The heavens, earth, and sea sing of the existence of the omniscient God. Psalm 53:1(NKJV) declares, "The fool has said in his heart there is no God." With so much proof of God as Creator in nature, it actually takes more effort to deny His existence than to simply look around and believe in Him.

To identify. When I'm asked to identify myself, I often show my driver's license. The picture and description announce to the inquisitor that it is indeed I who stands before him (give or take a few pounds). To identify God is to understand that it is He who goes before us and works in our situations—even the bad ones. When the Israelites were finally freed from the Egyptians, Moses led them out from Pharaoh's captivity. But Pharaoh gathered his army to pursue them. As confusion arose in the Egyptian camp, Pharaoh's soldiers identified God as the one who was protecting Israel. "Let's get away from the Israelites! The Lord is fighting for them against Egypt" (Exodus 14:25). Even as his army identified God as Israel's victor, Pharaoh refused to retreat. To his horror, he watched his entire army drown in the Red Sea. This miraculous work of God proved tragic to the pagan Pharaoh.

In Acts 22:7–8, we see the beginning of the transformation of Saul the persecutor of Christians into Paul the Apostle. Saul was blinded by a great light and fell to the ground. A voice said, "Saul, Saul, why are you persecuting me?" Saul's reply was, "Who are you, Lord?" He immediately identified the almighty presence of God, although he had not yet become acquainted with Him. These two examples remind us that God is present in every situation. Our choice is to ignore Him and walk in hardness of heart as Pharaoh did or seek His face and hunger to know Him better, like the man who came to be known as the apostle Paul. To identify God is to say, "God is in this situation somewhere," and then trust Him to show himself strong on our behalf.

To recognize. We have to look at God in order to recognize Him. Sounds simple, doesn't it? But people have always had trouble recognizing God as He moves on this earth. Jesus came to earth to show us God, and to declare Him (John 1:18). However, in John 14:9, Jesus told His own disciple, "Have I been so long with you and yet hast thou not known me Philip? He that hath seen me hath seen the Father." Jesus, who is God the Son, shone with the love, the wisdom, and the character of God the Father. As He walked the earth showing compassion and mercy, He showed us the nature of God. His sacrifice on the cross for our sin and His resurrection from the dead demonstrates to us God's plan for our redemption. To recognize God is to realize who Jesus is and what He came to do. "Jesus saith unto him, I am the way, the truth, and the life: no man cometh unto the Father, but by me" (John 14:6).

To have a relationship with. When we enter into a relationship with another, we tend to take interest in that person. We may spend time talking, engaging in common pursuits, and sharing meals together. One person often extends an invitation to the other, which is graciously accepted. A relationship of fellowship and mutual affection begins. God extends an invitation to all humanity. He wants to have a relationship with each of us. When Adam and Eve sinned in the garden, that fellowship was broken and was not fully restored until Jesus paid the penalty with His blood. Now He invites us to have uninterrupted friendship with Him. Jesus himself beckons us in Revelation 3:20, "Behold, I stand at the door and knock: if any man hear my voice and open the door, I will come in to him and will sup with him, and he with me." Unlike many of our human relationships, Jesus is calling us unconditionally, no matter who we are. "All that the Father giveth me shall come to me, and him that cometh to me I will in no wise cast out" (John 6:37). Our relationship with God involves accepting His son, Jesus, talking to Him in prayer, and listening to Him through quiet meditation in the Word of God. We'll find no greater friendship, no more fulfilling relationship, than with Jesus.

To have intimacy with. I have a best friend whom I'm so close with that we often know what the other is thinking. I can predict her reactions, and if I hear that she has done something out of character, I refuse to believe it. I say, "I know her. She wouldn't do a thing like that." In the Bible, Job knew God like that. He was intimate with God. Even though he was suffering horrendously, he maintained his faith in God because he knew Him. In the face of accusing friends and an unbelieving wife, Job kept his intimacy with God. "For I know that my redeemer liveth, and that he shall stand at the latter day upon the earth. And though after my skin worms destroy this body, yet in my flesh shall I see God" (Job 19:25–26).

Abraham had intimacy with God even when God asked him to sacrifice his son, Isaac. Abraham was so confident in God that he believed that God would raise Isaac again from the dead. God provided a ram for the sacrifice, but He also rewarded Abraham for his faith by making his offspring into a great nation (Genesis 22:1–19). Paul says of Abraham in Romans 4:20–21, "He staggered not at the promise of God through unbelief; but was strong in faith, giving glory to God; and being fully persuaded that, what he had promised, he was able also to perform."

To unite with. My parents were united in marriage in 1948. They raised five children and a grandchild in our home, and rarely, if ever, spent a night apart. They forged a united front in raising us—in discipline, affection, encouragement, and advice. They were *one.* After 37 years of marriage, my mother went to be with the Lord. My father was so grief-stricken he refused to eat, dress, or see visitors. Four months later, he died, literally of a broken heart. This is a true love story of a man who did not want to live without the love of his life. God wants us to be so united with Him through Jesus that we won't want to live without Him. He desires for us to say like Paul, "I count all things but loss for the excellency of the knowledge of Christ Jesus my Lord: for whom I have suffered the loss of all things, and do count them but dung, that I may win Christ" (Philippians 3:8).

My parents, as are many long-married couples, were often teased that they had been together so long they had begun to look alike. Now, looking at pictures, I can see some slight resemblance in their features. God wants us to look like Him, too. We were originally created in His image, which was tainted by sin. Nothing pleases God more than for His people to be in such close union with Him that we have His features. God's features are outlined in Galatians 5:22–23. They are love, joy, peace, longsuffering, gentleness, goodness, faith, meekness, and temperance. When others look at us, they should see these features of God. To unite with God means to refuse to live without Him, and to look, talk, and act like Him.

What are the advantages of knowing God?

1. **Protection**: "No weapon that is formed against thee shall prosper; and every tongue that shall rise against thee in judgment thou shalt condemn. This is the heritage of the servants of the Lord; and their righteousness is of me, saith the Lord" (Isaiah 54:7).

2. **Power**: "Now unto him that is able to do exceeding abundantly above all that we ask or think, according to the power that worketh in us" (Ephesians 3:20).

3. **Guidance**: "In all thy ways acknowledge him, and he shall direct thy paths" (Proverbs 3:6).

4. **Peace**: "Peace I leave with you, my peace I give unto you, not as the world giveth give I unto you. Let not your heart be troubled, neither let it be afraid" (John 14:27).

Know God. Notice Him in everything. Recognize His hand working. Enter into relationship with Him through Jesus Christ. Become intimate with His character and His Word. Unite with Him so others can see Christ in you. It's not what you know; it's *whom* you know.

CHAPTER 21

Going All the Way

"And it came to pass, that when Jesus had finished these sayings, He departed from Galilee, and came into the coasts of Judea beyond Jordan. And great multitudes followed him; and he healed them there."

(Matthew 19:1-2)

At quick glance, these verses seem to merely be a geographical guide to set a background for the subsequent text. They move the reader from the deep spiritual teaching about brotherly love found in Matthew 18 to the commands for family life in chapter 19. However, every word of Scripture is filled with Spirit, power, and life. These verses are not just transition sentences, but contain the revelation of spiritual truth.

Notice that Jesus had been with the great multitudes in Capernaum for quite some time—to pay a tax with the money from the fish's mouth (Matthew 17:24-27), to tell the parable about an unforgiving servant (Matthew 18:23-35), and to teach many other life lessons. He could have healed those people at any point during His teachings. There were undoubtedly people in the crowd who were waiting for Jesus to heal them. It appears from the gospel record that Jesus had a particular plan for this group.

Matthew 19:1 tells us about the trip the multitudes took with Jesus. They walked from Galilee through Samaria to Judea—a very, very long walk—at least 40 miles. The next verse (19:2) tells us that Jesus healed them *there*. There is no mention of Jesus healing people along the way or of Him healing anyone who hadn't stayed with Him for the whole journey. Only those who went all the way with Jesus were healed.

Throughout the Word of God there are examples of healings performed, not instantaneously, but through a process. Job's recovery began after he obediently prayed for his friends (Job 42:10). The ten lepers were cleansed as they obeyed Jesus and walked toward the temple to show themselves to the priests (Luke 17:12–19). A blind man's sight returned after Jesus put mud on his eyes and commanded him to wash in the pool of Siloam (John 9:1–7). These, and countless others received healings as they responded in faith and obedience to God's commands.

The multitudes following Jesus went beyond the Jordan. They had to use this river and even cross it at some point in their walk with Jesus. The Jordan River was known as the muddiest river in the region. It was not popular for people to plunge into the dirty waters of the Jordan. Recall Naaman, the great captain of Syria, who had contracted leprosy (2 Kings 5:9–14). He thought surely the prophet Elisha would just pray for him and heal him. Instead, he was instructed to wash in the Jordan River seven times. Naaman, feeling he was above dipping himself in such filthy water, suggested other rivers he would rather use. However, it wasn't until he humbly submitted to God's plan that he was healed.

There are many muddy rivers in our lives—situations we would rather not face, faults we would prefer to conceal, and circumstances we attempt to avoid. Jesus wants to walk us through these muddy waters to reach the healing on the other side. Just as the multitudes stayed with Jesus through the muddy Jordan, He wants us to persevere through the rough spots on our faith walk with Him.

There is no mention in Matthew 19:1–2 that Jesus announced what the final destination would be, how long the trip would take, or what might happen along the way. The multitudes simply kept their eyes on Jesus, listened to His voice, and faithfully followed Him. *(Read that sentence again and be blessed!)* It was only at the end of that particular walk that the people were healed.

"Many are the afflictions of the righteous, but the Lord delivereth him out of them all" (Psalm 34:19). We can trust our Lord to answer our needs for healing, deliverance, wisdom, fulfillment, guidance, and every other request we have. How and when He chooses to answer is according to His plan. Like this group who followed Jesus, we may not receive until we have walked obediently, listened faithfully to His Word, and patiently crossed some muddy waters of affliction or testing.

Whether we seek spiritual, emotional, or physical healing, the faith walk with Jesus will lead us to the place of recovery. We must make it all the way with Jesus, seeking His wisdom, sitting under His teaching, and letting Him walk us through our muddy Jordans. "Commit your way to the Lord, trust also in Him, and He shall bring it to pass" (Psalm 37:5, NKJV).

CHAPTER 22

Survive or Live?

I recently saw a preview of a reality television show called *Survival*. Apparently this show involves contestants being placed on an island or out in the wilderness to fend for themselves. These people put themselves in uncomfortable and even frightening circumstances *on purpose* to see who will come away from the challenge the winner (or in one piece).

Life tends to play survival games on us too—except it's not a game. Tragedy happens, disappointments occur, people say and do things to make us wonder how we will ever survive. If I were to ask a number of people if they would like to survive every problem they face, the majority of individuals would probably say yes. But, God does not want us to survive. He wants us to *live!*

There is a tremendous distinction between surviving and living. By definition, to survive means to remain alive, or to outlive. This description places an image in my mind of someone dragging along, scarred, bruised, and beaten down, but still managing to keep on breathing. The destiny of God's people is not to wait out the drudgery of this life in hope of somehow crawling into glory. The word *survive* is found nowhere in the Bible. No, God wants infinitely more for his people. The purpose of Jesus coming to this earth was to give us abundant life (John 10:10).

The word *live* means to continue, to endure, to last, to prevail, or to remain. This gives the impression that we stand strong after each struggle, as victors, not as wounded puppies, but better than we were before the trouble began. The third chapter of Daniel tells us about three young Hebrews who were captives in Babylon. Verses 15–18 report how these young men made a stand in the face of the enemy who threatened to throw them in the furnace if they didn't bow to the king. Standing firm in their convictions, they refused to bow before anyone but Almighty God. They were bound and thrown into the furnace, heated seven times its normal temperature. Not only did these young men live, but according to Daniel 3:27, they came through with no signs of struggle—no burns, no singes, not even the smell of smoke! "Then Nebuchadnezzar the king was astonished, and rose up in haste, and spake, and said unto his counselors, Did not we cast three men bound into the midst of the fire? They answered and said unto the king, True, O king. He answered and said, Lo, I see four men loose, walking in the midst of the fire, and they have no hurt, and the form of the fourth is like the Son of God" (Daniel 3:24–25)." These young men didn't just survive their punishment, they lived; they prevailed! Why? The Lord Jesus Christ was with them in the furnace!

Likewise, as children of the Living God, we can be assured that our Lord is with us. We can know that we can *live* this life, not just survive it. He promises that we shall not be destroyed if we walk in fellowship and obedience to Him.

"When you pass through the waters, I will be with you; And through the rivers, they shall not overflow you. When you walk through the fire, you shall not be burned, nor shall the flame scorch you" (Isaiah 43:2, NKJV). This promise brings peace, comfort, and security for those who trust God at His word. However, this pledge is not intended for those who refuse to honor God and instead walk according to their own desires and plans. God expects those who enter the promise of life through Jesus Christ to walk faithfully with Him. Thus, this and all the other promises in God's Word will be available to whoever stays in communion and fellowship with Him.

How do we walk with God and live? One way is through **communication** with Him. God is delighted when we seek His face, and He is eager to answer us. (Psalm 86:7). When we talk to God and stop to listen, He will respond to us. His voice may come in the form of a thought, a verbal message through someone else, or it may be confirmed through circumstances. Most importantly, as Jesus tells us in John 6:63, "The words that I speak unto you, they are spirit, and they are life." God's Word is life. When we read, study, and meditate in God's Word, it will come back to memory to direct us in every situation life brings. "But the Comforter, which is the Holy Ghost, whom the Father will send in my name, he shall teach you all things, and bring all things to your remembrance, whatsoever I have said unto you" (John 14:26).

Another vital component in walking with God is **obedience**. We've got to do it God's way. "My sheep hear my voice, and I know them, and they follow me: And I give unto them eternal life; and they shall never perish, neither shall any man pluck them out of my hand" (John 10:27–28). Life comes from following Jesus. In fact, Jesus announces himself as "The Life" in John 14:6. A person who does not live in obedience to Christ is not really living at all. Romans 4:4 tells us that we were once dead in our sins, but now we should walk in the newness of life in Christ. The book of Proverbs is dedicated to differentiating between the life of obedient wisdom and the folly of the disobedient fool. *The book of Proverbs is one of my favorites. It is hard to put down, profoundly relevant to modern life, and crystal clear in its message.*

The difference between surviving and living can be found throughout the pages of God's Word. Don't go through life being just a survivor—**LIVE!**

CHAPTER 23

We're On a Roll!

I often look through my kitchen window as I am washing dishes and watch my twins playing in the back yard with their friends. Occasionally, I can watch a kickball game in its entirety (or until somebody gets mad and goes home). I notice that when they kick from the top of the hill, the ball rolls much farther and faster. Now, I didn't glean much from my sixth-grade science class, but I do remember that the forces of gravity and inertia allow the ball to roll better downhill than up.

We might use the phrase "we're on a roll" when referring to some encouraging progression. This statement indicates a continuation of the current progress and ultimate achievement of a goal. Essentially, inertia has taken effect, and the plan for success is working.

Every human being that has ever lived was born "on a roll." We were each formed in God's image and given gifts and talents to walk in a course of life designed for us. Even before birth, each of us was given a temperament and certain physical and intellectual tendencies that God helps us develop throughout life. In Psalm 139:13–16, David recognizes that God knew us before we were born. Jeremiah 29:11 declares that God's plans for us are all good. The Word of God confirms that from the development of our first cell, God has a plan for every person.

Since we're "on a roll" from birth, the difference between rolling uphill or downhill depends upon the choices we make. Obviously, rolling downhill is much easier and more popular than rolling uphill. Jesus explains this in Matthew 7:13–14, "Enter ye at the strait gate; for wide is the gate, and broad is the way that leadeth to destruction, and many there be that go in thereat. Because strait is the gate and narrow is the way which leadeth unto life, and few there be that find it." The narrow, upward path is less populated, and the wide, downward path is crowded because of its ease.

In life, rolling downward refers to our natural tendency to sin (Romans 3:23), walking in our fleshly desires (Galatians 5:19–21), and our carnal rebellion against God working in our lives (Galatians 5:17). Jesus gives us an illustration in Luke 12:16–21 of a man who lived a life of ease and luxury but forgot God. In his godless complacency, he heard the words from the Lord, "Thou fool, this night your soul shall be required of thee . . . ." That man, more interested in the things of this world, forfeited his eternity, rejected the upward climb to glory, and lost his soul.

Living a Christian life is not easy. We are constantly lured by the flesh, the world, and the devil. The resounding voices of "if it feels good, do it," "be the best, beat the rest," and the "me" philosophies that have infiltrated our society have sought to quiet the still, small voice that speaks in the spirit. Yes, rolling upward is difficult to do. We need help, a force strong enough to overcome the spiritual gravity that plagues this world. We have help. Jesus introduces us to our help in John 16:13, "Howbeit when he, the Spirit of truth is come, he will guide you into all truth . . . he will show you things to come." The Holy Spirit resides in the believer to assist us up the path to a godly life and an eternity in heaven.

The apostle Paul was on an upward roll. He rejoiced as he faithfully executed his calling. But he was met with trouble in nearly every city he visited. He was beaten, jailed, falsely accused, chained, and verbally abused. But he realized that his suffering could not compare to the glory he would see in heaven. That's how he could say in 2 Corinthians 4:8–9, "We are troubled on every side, yet not distressed; we are perplexed, but not in despair; persecuted, but not forsaken; cast down, but not destroyed."

Yes, we're on a roll. The direction we're rolling, rather downward to destruction and hell or upward to righteousness and heaven, depends solely on what we decide to do with Jesus. If we ignore Him, we'll be separated from Him forever. If we follow Him and trust Him, we'll find joy on this earth and we'll live with Him forever. Roll on!

CHAPTER 24

Live in the Light

Some days are sunny and warm; some are rainy and gloomy. Some are gray and stormy; others are cold and windy. No matter what the meteorological description, this revolving segment of time is still called *day*. The explanation for that (if I remember my 4th grade science) is that our side of the earth is facing the sun. From the sun comes light, so there we have it—day.

At the risk of sounding corny, I will relate the sunlight to the *Sonlight* (follow me here—I promise to take you somewhere). When we face the Son, we receive light, even on the darkest, gloomiest of days.

Jesus is God the Son, and He wants us to turn to Him for light. "I have come as a light into the world, that whoever believes in me should not abide in darkness (John 12:46, NKJV). Jesus here explains that He is light, available for the entire world to come to Him for eternal life.

It bears out in Scripture that those who faced God radiated His light. In Exodus 34:28–35, Moses had met God on Mount Sinai to receive the Ten Commandments. As he descended from the mountain, the people were astonished at his appearance. The Israelites hid their faces from him because of the brightness of his glowing skin. Jesus met with God the Father on the Mount of Transfiguration. Peter, James, and John watched the stunning brightness engulf Jesus as Moses and Elijah suddenly appeared and spoke with Him (Matthew 17:1–3). Saul, who later became the apostle Paul, was actually blinded by the light of God when he was changed on the Damascus Road (Acts 9:3–9).

Facing the *Son* means coming into personal contact with Jesus. Coming into the *light* changes a life forever! Recall Moses, who before his encounter, had been an exile hiding in the desert. Yes, he obeyed as God delivered the plagues to the Egyptians, but with much trembling and uncertainty. In fact, he hadn't even been courageous enough to speak to the Pharaoh himself but needed his brother Aaron to speak for him (Exodus 4:10–16). But after he was bathed in the light of God's powerful presence, he became one of the greatest, boldest leaders in biblical history. Peter, James, and John were witnesses to the great light, and after seeing it, they were committed to a course that eventually led them to become fervent preachers—Peter, the stone (John 1:42), and James and John, the sons of thunder (Mark 3:17). Paul, after his encounter with the light, set out with relentless abandon to change the world for Christ.

When we face the Son, it means we are turning away from darkness. Like the earth, we cannot face the light and darkness at the same time. In 1 Peter 2:9 we find that we have been called "out of darkness and into His marvelous light." To face the Son, we must turn our backs on everything dark or unlike God. Some examples of darkness would be:

1. *Fear:* "For God hath not given us the spirit of fear: but of power, and of love, and of a sound mind" (2 Timothy 1:7).

2. *Depression:* "To appoint unto them that mourn in Zion, to give unto them beauty for ashes, the oil of joy for mourning, the garment of praise for the spirit of heaviness: that they might be called trees of righteousness, the planting of the Lord, that He might be glorified" (Isaiah 61:3).

3. *Anxiety:* "Be careful for nothing; but in everything by prayer and supplication with thanksgiving let your requests be made known unto God. And the peace of God, which passeth all understanding, shall keep your hearts and minds through Christ Jesus" (Philippians 4:6–7).

4. *Selfishness:* "For the flesh lusteth against the Spirit, and the Spirit against the flesh: and these are contrary the one to the other: so ye cannot do the things that ye would" (Galatians 5:17).

Living in the light will cause us to grow in the Lord. No longer shall we be "me, me, me" spiritual babies. No, as we walk with the Son, we shall mature in Him, thinking of others more than ourselves (Philippians 2:3). As we grow in the Lord, we begin to recognize dangers such as false teachers that try to deceive us.

What does light do? Think about it. When we walk into a room with no lights, it's dark, and maybe a little scary. Whether we have a candle, flashlight, lamp, or spotlight, the more light there is, the less darkness there can be. As the light increases, the darkness becomes only shadows. And who's ever been hurt by a shadow? In 1 John 4:4, we are reminded that greater is He that is in us (light) than he that is in the world (darkness).

When we turn on a light, we can see where we are going; we won't stumble or trip over obstacles in our way. Psalm 119:105 "Thy Word is a lamp unto my feet and a light unto my path." Living in the light is the way to get God's purpose accomplished in our lives. Just as driving a car with the headlights on illuminates a dark street, living in the light will make what appeared to be a dead end become an open road for our success.

Light makes us winners. When an enemy launches an attack in the dark, he has the upper hand. Our enemy, the devil, often attacks us in our darkness (our own pride, fear, doubt, etc.). This way, he can hide behind our justifications for our sin ("I'm only human," "This is just the way I am") and maintain an element of surprise. We rarely see it coming when suddenly the enemy is upon us, and we find ourselves in battle. Truly, we shall have battles in our lives, but if we live in the light we'll know who the enemy is (Ephesians 6:12), we'll know what to do (Ephesians 6:13), and we'll know who is going to win (Romans 8:37)!

Face the Son. Walk in His light. Live to win. Talk to Him. Read His Word. Seek relationships with other Christians.

"But if we walk in the light, as he is in the light, we have fellowship with one another, and the blood of Jesus Christ, his son, cleanses us from all sin" (1 John 1:7, NKJV).

WOMAN OF DESTINY

Throughout each age of time revealed
The plan of God has been fulfilled
Through gentle vessels, meek yet bold,
Whose stories of faith are still being told.

These women of God, with honor and grace,
In annals of history each has a place.
Whether Deborah, or Anna, or Esther, or Ruth,
These women of power each walked in the truth.

Mary and Martha, who talked with our Lord;
We shall always recall it was He they adored.
And the mother of Jesus, as soon as she heard,
Said "yes" to the Father, obeying His Word.

When the call of the Father is heard in your heart,
Like those women of old, you stand up, do your part.
Be faithful and trusting, God won't let you fail.
You're a woman of destiny, let His Will prevail.

". . . and who knoweth whether thou has come to the Kingdom for such a time as this?"
Esther 4:14

Special thanks to:

My pastor, Rev. Dr. Roland Hayes Crowder, whose kind words and encouragement have built me up in the faith.

Pastor Ron and Jan Dress, who taught me how to study and grow from God's Word.

Eva Betz, and John and Toni Sobolewski, who discipled me back in the early days, and spent countless hours worshipping God with me.

Mary Jo, Renee, Bessie, and Vivian, the best friends a girl could have.

My church family, who saw something in me I didn't realize I had.

Mom and Dad, the late Rev. John and Betty Medley; I know you're smiling.

Especially to you, my Lord Jesus Christ, my Savior, my all.

To order additional copies of

Dialogue
WITH THE MASTER
LIFE LESSONS FOR THE GROWING CHRISTIAN

Have your credit card ready and call:

1-877-421-READ (7323)

or please visit our web site at
www.pleasantword.com

Also available at:
www.amazon.com
and
www.barnesandnoble.com

Printed in the United States
75848LV00001B/403-498